HERSCHEL

HERSCHEL

The Boy Who Started World War II

Andy Marino

Faber and Faber

BOSTON • LONDON

© Andy Marino 1995

Library of Congress Cataloging-in-Publication Data

Marino, Andy.
    Herschel : the boy who started World War II /
by Andy Marino.
        p.   cm.
    ISBN 0-571-19921-6
    1. Grynszpan, Herschel Feibel, 1921–ca. 1943.   2. Jews—
Germany—Hannover—Biography.   3. Jews—Germany—
History—1933–1945.   4. Refugees, Jewish—France—Paris—
Biography.   5. Assassins—France—Paris—Biography.
6. Germany—Ethnic relations.   I. Title.
DS135.G3315M38   1997
943.086′092—dc21   97-14168
    [B]   CIP
                                                    r97

Jacket design by Ha Nguyen

Printed in the United States of America

CONTENTS

ACKNOWLEDGEMENTS

Books always look as though they are the singular work of the author, but it is my experience, at least, that putting the words on paper is just part of it.

So naturally there are several important people to whom I owe a great debt of thanks. Looming largest among them is Richard 'Two Breakfasts' Gollner, my literary agent in London. I would also like to thank Neil Hornick, a careful and gentle reader, and an excellent critic; and Anna Swan, whose dead-eye proof-reading was so impressive and intelligent, and who made all the difference in more ways than one.

It was Steven Berkoff's passionate custodianship of Herschel's memory that led to a short film monologue about him. This was directed by my good friend Gerry Troyna, who in turn introduced me to this strange story.

In the United States, I would like to thank Albert Zuckerman, at Writers House, and Dan Weaver, at Faber & Faber, who both liked this book well enough to get behind it.

Herschel Grynszpan, though young and ill-used by fate, seems to have had a talent for entering and enriching the lives of others. So, if he is still alive and out there, I'd like to thank him as well.

INTRODUCTION

One fine morning Joseph K, the hero of Kafka's novel, *The Trial*, awoke to find that somebody had been telling lies about him. The proof of this was the figure standing by his bed, in the shape of a policeman who had come to arrest him. Without warning or explanation Joseph K had become a criminal, and found his existence redefined by others he had never met. Faced with an enveloping nightmare, he accepted the shady jurisdiction of the faceless judge, and came increasingly to rely on his 'case' as both reason and explanation for his very existence. Once one is so entwined, or hooked, the unexplained and spurious legality of the persecutor is authenticated and granted its powers by the accused himself. Then there's no hope.

In the novel Joseph K dutifully turns up every day to petition various functionaries for hearings, to plead with disinterested bureaucrats. Being told that co-operation and diligence will help him, he pathetically seeks to appease the court, whose malignity he can never fully comprehend or believe. In addition to keeping him captive, in both the physical and psychological sense, this attitude implicitly grants the faceless judge the power of sentence, and as a result Joseph K dies, finished off, 'Like a dog!'

But imagine that, instead of admitting the court's power over him, Joseph K resisted. He was yet young and unformed, fascinated with the world and full of plans for his future. Suppose that after hearing he was accused, and suspecting that his crime could not be revealed to him because in fact there was none, the charges being cooked up by an invisible foe, Joseph K made himself disappear. Suppose eventually he realised the evil and aggressiveness of the dark forces ranged against him and knew he could not escape. Suppose, finally, that one fine morning, unannounced, Joseph K walked into the court itself and shot dead the judge. Suppose all that and you have the bare bones of the life of Herschel Grynszpan, a German Jew who grew up at exactly the same time as the Nazi Party, and whose coming of age was coterminal with the beginning of the Holocaust.

The Trial is maybe the essential twentieth century story, for it insists how obscure and unimportant is each of us in a bureaucratic age, and thus how susceptible we are to the flattery of our own psychological policeman. Paranoia is our state of mind, for at least it enables us to feel significant. A grey little nobody, Joseph K grew obsessed with justice because he simply did not have a life of his own worth living. His 'case' was a gift, an excuse, the most interesting thing about him; so perhaps he deserved and even wanted what he got. But Kafka's novel is also a prophetic political parable. To a German Jew in the 1930's, the circumstances and logic of the illogical state machinery behind Joseph K's persecution would have been uncannily familiar. These people were living a reality of hell, not some literary parable. They did not seek what they received from the Nazis.

Herschel's story, then, is of a young Jew who fought back; of a boy who, denying the dire authority of his criminal government, personally declared war on Hitler. Herschel's actions refute the notion that The Court is all powerful and unassailable, and though his story is but a small element in the huge mosaic of heroism and resistance against Hitler's diabolical régime, it is one which remains unique and significant. It seems to encapsulate the larger movements of history and condense them into emblematic form. Sir Michael Tippett certainly felt this when he composed *A Child of our Time* (in 1941-2, and for which Edith Sitwell wrote the libretto), and spoke of how the events of the shooting and its aftermath were transformed into general and almost mythological significance.[1]

The subtitle of this book is 'The Boy Who Started World War II', a claim that, were it taken literally, would not stand up for a moment before any historian. Yet when Herschel walked into the German embassy in Paris, one fine morning in November 1938, he knew only that Hitler was already at war, if not as yet with the world, then certainly with Herschel and his family, because they had made the mistake of being Jewish. In March of 1938 Hitler had engineered the Anschluss with Austria and absorbed it within the greater German Reich. He was now involved with the partitioning of Czechoslovakia, and aiming for the complete destruction of that nation. In the meantime, and for the last six years, Hitler had been persecuting Jews, gypsies, homosexuals, 'asocial elements' and left-wingers in his own country. But most of all he had been persecuting the Jews.

At the behest of his terrified family, Herschel had fled Germany and eventually taken refuge in Paris, where as an illegal alien he was sought by the police. A stateless fugitive with no way home, Herschel was nearing the end of his tether when he received a postcard from his distraught family relating how they had been expelled from Germany back to their notional homeland of Poland. The Poles, no friends of the Jews, were reluctant to allow them in, and the Grynszpans, with thousands of other Jews, were sitting helplessly in a borderline no-man's land.

Unlike the governments of Britain and France, Herschel read the writing on the wall. He saw that international appeasement was exactly what suited Hitler best. Above all, Herschel saw into Hitler's black heart and knew what the dictator was planning. In a desperate attempt to alert the world to the plight of the Jews, 'his people',

Herschel conceived of a desperate act that would force the sluggish foreign powers to act against the manifest brutality of the Nazis. Herschel walked into the German embassy and shot a young official called Ernst vom Rath. The wounded vom Rath died two days later, and immediately afterwards the pogrom known as Kristallnacht was unleashed against the Jews in Germany.

Initially, Herschel was blamed by friend and foe alike for the atrocities inflicted on the Jews in Germany. But slowly opinion shifted. It transpired that Kristallnacht, like so much else in Hitler's evil game, had been planned and prepared for. Herschel had merely forced the führer's hand. His action had the effect of flushing out the Nazis from their cover of political respectibility and peaceful intentions. They stood revealed as power-hungry maniacs and thugs who idolised 'cheerful brutality', and scorned tolerance as weakness. Herschel's act delayed the signing of the Franco-German friendship pact, which was under preparation at the time, by only one month.[2] As such, the discernable political consequences were minor. Nevertheless, in the interim the Western democracies were forced to re-evaluate Hitler's plans and motives, and their own responses to them.

Herschel forced the Western powers to contemplate their own moral complacency and, just as importantly, the practical implications of a war it could not be denied was fast approaching. During Herschel's pre-trial incarceration, the fate of Poland was decided in meetings between Germany and the Soviet Union, and the Allies were forced to make a stand, thus effectively guaranteeing World War II was on schedule. Herschel was in no way the cause of these later events, but he had encouraged Hitler to come clean about his international and diplomatic desires. The führer honestly affirmed he was not interested in negotiation and friendship, but only in a war of conquest.

Hitler was keen for conflict in any case, before his enemies-to-be caught up to German levels of rearmament, and before (he believed) his precarious health failed. Chance would have been a fine thing. But again, Herschel's pre-emptive strike visibly speeded up Hitler's aggressive manœuvres; it forced the little dictator, whose neighbours were by now alarmed, to go to war before Germany was fully prepared. In the end, this may well have had some decisive influence on the outcome of World War II. For example, Hitler's navy, by the time he was at the Channel coast, was too small to launch an invasion of the British Isles. On his Mediterranean flank there was weakness, for his ally Mussolini had warned that the Italians were not yet prepared for war.[3] Feeling harried and hurried, Hitler struck too early and too deeply into Russia, and when soon after his unbalanced recklessness led him to declare war on the United States, the European conflict was effectively on the turn, even if it did not yet appear so.

Once again, Herschel cannot take any of the credit for this. I do not even believe the claim that, but for Herschel's desperate act, the opening shots of the Second World War might have been in the east, possibly even averting a world war and sparing Western Europe altogether. In reality Hitler not only wanted the security of a solid western flank on the European mainland, unthreatened by France and Britain, but he also needed the raw materials of the countries he invaded, not least the Scandinavian ones, to have any hope of prosecuting a successful offensive against Stalin. One consequence of Herschel's action was to make this fact clear, and sooner than it otherwise would have been.

Above all, though, the claim that Herschel started World War II refers to the person this book is about. Possessing a clairvoyance and farsightedness at the time not shared, or at least not acted on, by any other figure or power in Europe, Herschel decided to declare war himself. After his crime, Herschel acted with military aggressiveness, eventually managing to defeat Hitler's plans for him from within a concentration camp. He knew his life was forfeit from the beginning, even from before he fired the shots from his revolver. Herschel believed he had nothing to lose, so he went to war, and there is sufficient evidence to support the argument that in a sense he won.

There exist already two exhaustive, sincere and factually accurate accounts of the Herschel Grynszpan affair. The first, an unpublished thesis, was written in the early nineteen-sixties by Alain Cuenot, a French doctor, the origin of whose interest in the story is slightly puzzling, but which has been useful for anybody interested in this sad but significant tale. It is written with a scientist's detachment and a cold passion that relentlessly censures the young Jewish assassin, yet to my mind contains something of a bereaved father's love for an errant son. (It is almost as if Cuenot is apologising to the Jews, on behalf of the French, for Herschel's crime and its consequences) He remains convinced that Herschel's action was counter-productive, and that the boy himself was a megalomaniac, almost a reflection of Hitler himself. Though it must be granted that there were elements of immaturity and egotism in Herschel's personality, I fundamentally disagree with Dr Cuenot. The circumstances surrounding Herschel's crime more than exonerate the boy from these charges, and indeed I attempt to argue just how mature and intelligent Herschel's behaviour, both before and after the shooting, really was. Above all, Cuenot seems to forget just how normal Herschel was, as a seventeen year-old (one blushes to recall oneself at that age), and one under almost unprecedented pressures. In the decisions about his life that Herschel consciously took, and in his spiritual resolve thereafter, he was surely an extraordinary figure, a lone voice of anger and vengeance in a cowed and shoddy collection of democracies.

The author of the second study of the Herschel Grynszpan affair, Gerald Schwab, is more equable in his attitude to the boy. Schwab is an American citizen and former US diplomat, who in a previous life had suffered as a Jewish boy under the Nazi régime in pre-war Germany. He lived through Kristallnacht before escaping to the States and later fought his way back into his former homeland. Had he not fled Germany when he did, he would probably have been exterminated, as he well knows. For Schwab, it is easier to look on Herschel as a lifesaver, despite the suffering that his crime precipitated. Later, Schwab worked as an interpreter at the Nuremburg trials, and his book, *The Day The Holocaust Began* (1989), is already history beginning to be transformed into drama: a measured, calm but deadly account that locates the story of Herschel more widely in the context of the totalitarian sickness that was Nazism, and which has no qualms about choosing sides and settling scores. Schwab's are some of the final shots of the war – that second attempt at what F Scott-Fitzgerald called (with chilling finesse) the 'delayed Teutonic migration'.

For the more serious student of history I would recommend Schwab's book over Cuenot's (which anyway is difficult to obtain), not because it has more facts – though it does – but because it is more readable. Both writers make full use of the mass of documentation surrounding the case: contemporary newspaper reports, depositions and research pertaining to the trial, eye-witness accounts, letters, postcards, rumours and anecdotes, all impeccably weighed according to each author's lights. Their energies are disposed towards a full review of the facts, and as such their conclusions, though final in certain regards, remain provisional in an academic sense. That is no criticism, by the way.

So I think there is room for another book, one that attempts less to document every scrap of paper pertinent to the affair, and more to tell the story as just that. This is, for want of a better term, a work of historical journalism. It observes the academic conventions, and the facts related are documented facts, with references to where they were found. But I am also trying to render shapely, in the way the moral of a novel informs its shapeliness, the bare facts of history: it has heroes and villains, and no apology is made for that. My story also owes a great debt to the labours of Schwab and Cuenot. I do, however, disagree with them on many points, and in Cuenot's example with the overall attitude. In the course of addressing the facts of the case I also found myself arguing certain theories that neither Schwab nor Cuenot allows himself to contemplate. The most important concerns the secret identity of Herschel's victim, Baron Ernst vom Rath, and the way in which he truly met his end. Once we understand exactly who Herschel attacked, the tragedy of the tale is yet further deepened.

Lastly, may I say that while researching and writing this book, it again came clear just how barbaric, for all its culture and achievements, Europe really is. It has been one of the bloodiest killing fields of the world, either actively or (thinking of the Cold War) latently. This history is not yet concluded. One of the most depressing and nauseating things that hit home about the Herschel Grynszpan story was how contemporary and familiar it felt. The obvious parallel, which surfaces in the mind even as one tries to suppress it, was the conflict in the former Yugoslavia. There, little Hitlers obsessed with racial purity once again strutted along their battlements. A hamstrung and sheepish collection of free governments (for The League of Nations read The United Nations) looked helplessly on, alternatively appeasing the murderers or issuing laughable threats. Ethnic 'cleansing' took place, with people being swept into the sewers of new concentration camps. Stateless refugees, like Herschel Grynszpan, helplessly watched their families perish. Though quiet now, it is by no means over. How long will it be before another child, driven to some new single act of desperation, plunges the peaceful world into the turbulent waters of a further conflict which might then spread, like a dark poisonous flood, across the civilised homeland of Europe?

Andy Marino
London, January 1997

PROLOGUE

Hanover, 28 October 1938

The family were sitting down to supper when the knock at the door came, hard and loud. The policeman – the 'Shupo' – told them it was necessary to visit the police station with their passports. There was no need to take anything else. Everyone would be travelling straight back home. But when the family – parents, son and daughter – arrived at Precinct 11, they found to their astonishment almost the entire neighbourhood collected there. The round-up had started early, and even children had been arrested, as they stepped from the schoolyard. Now there was clamour and wailing of women, the whimpers of confused children sensing the fear of the grown-ups.

Everyone had a paper to sign, an expulsion order declaring that their residence in Germany had been summarily terminated. These people were no longer 'considered worthy, because of their personality, of the hospitality accorded them'. Esther Grynszpan begged to be allowed to return home to pack some clothes, and she left, accompanied by a Shupo who stood over her as she threw a few garments into a valise. There was no time to rescue money or valuables from their safe places. Back at Precinct 11, one man had refused to sign the papers, and stood in the corner, his back to the room.[1]

Crowds lined the streets shouting 'Back to Palestine!' as they left the police station, and later a whole neighbourhood – nearly 600 people – was herded into a local beer-hall. There it remained for a night and a day, until late Friday. Then the Jews were loaded on trains. True to their word, the Germans were sending them home; but to Poland, where only the old had been born. At dawn this one community of many arrived at the border. Other trains, from all over Germany – from Leipzig, Berlin, Düsseldorf, Bremen, Cologne – were also terminating there. Everybody was searched, their money and jewelry confiscated. 'When you arrived you had only 10 marks; there's no reason for you to leave with more than that,' they were told. Soon 12,000 souls were being bullwhipped and chased by the SS through the woodland to the Polish border. The cold rain was heavy and the ground soft. Old men stumbled and fainted away, and were carried by the younger. One or two remained where they fell. Sendel Grynszpan collapsed, but his son hoisted him across his shoulder. 'Come, Papa, let's run,' he said, 'otherwise they will kill you.'[2] There was blood on the road.

Alarmed by the horde rushing towards them, the Polish guards fired rifle volleys over the heads of the refugees, until they saw the women and children who were approaching ahead of their men. Eventually the wretched travellers were allowed to leave one country that did not want them, only to enter another that felt the same way. The one building large enough to lodge them in was a military stables, and there they remained, cramped and lying in hunger on straw, lower than beasts in their suffering.

On Sunday a truck with bread arrived from Poznan, and those strong enough to fight for it received a crust. For the Grynszpans it was the first food since the interrupted meal on Thursday night.

Dimly, in their shock, the Jews started to realise what had begun.

Paris, 7 November 1938

The citizens of Paris were enjoying an Indian summer, and the morning of 7 November was especially bright and warm. François Autret, the gendarme on duty outside the German embassy on the rue de Lille, smartly saluted the ambassador, Count Johannes von Welczeck, as he emerged from the building slightly earlier than usual to take his morning constitutional. The Count nodded briefly to the policeman, consulted his fobwatch, and squinted with satisfaction at the welcoming sun. Then he noticed a youth talking with Autret, and the policeman gesturing down the street. Not following the policeman's directions, the youth – an extremely slight figure, dark and Mediterranean-looking – strode up the embassy steps just as Welczeck stepped out. 'Excuse me,' enquired the young man of the Count in perfect German, 'but is it possible to see His Excellency the Ambassador?'

The ambassador, a rather formal nineteenth-century personage, was embarrassed and irritated by the impudence of the youth's enquiry, and merely waved him in the direction of the reception area before hurrying into the busy street.

Once inside, the youth asked Mme Mathis, wife of the concierge, to direct him to the office of an embassy official. She happily showed the boy up one flight of stairs after being told that he had some papers to deliver. Herr Nagorka, the receptionist who received him, was annoyed at the young man, whose ignorance of protocol was clear. There were many officials working at the embassy, but at just after half-past nine in the morning not many were yet at their desks. The youth had no idea which official he wanted, and was talkative and nervous. In addition, he looked Jewish, like others of his kind who had been bombarding the embassy of late with their hysterical requests for visas and passports.

Nagorka demanded the nature of his visit, but the young man only declared, and then repeated, that he had important papers to deliver. He must, he insisted, hand them over personally. After a few minutes, the receptionist wearily ushered him into the waiting room and then disappeared down the corridor to see who was in. Sometimes, if an arrival was carrying 'certain documents', it was wise to neglect formality and show him into the office of the relevant official. And in the case of semitic-looking German speakers, the relevant official was Baron Ernst vom Rath. The young Baron was a diligent man, customarily one of the first officials to arrive at work.

Vom Rath had his back to his desk when the receptionist knocked on his door, and was sitting, thoughtfully looking out of the window at the sunny street and at the trees with their oddly bare branches. 'Enter,' he called, and Nagorka explained the situation. Vom Rath swivelled around in his chair and pursed his lips. He was a tall, lean man, and his skin was stretched tightly across his face. He looked like he had been unwell: malarial or even tubercular. He nodded as if he knew what it was about. 'Send him in,' said vom Rath. The receptionist returned to the grim-faced youth in the waiting-room and led him to vom Rath's office. He showed the boy in, noticing that the young Baron once more had his back to the room, and then left, closing the door behind him.

A few moments later Nagorka heard five sharp cracks, and he wondered for an instant what they were. He and Herr Kreuger, the other receptionist, exchanged a glance. But they had already realised exactly what the noises signified, and found themselves sprinting the thirty yards back down the corridor to vom Rath's office. When they got there vom Rath was leaning on the doorjamb, and behind him in the office was the youth, white-faced and visibly trembling. 'I am wounded,' said vom Rath in a calm voice, before he sat down on the floor.

The Vosges Mountains, December 1939

It was late at night when a police officer arrived at the school-house of Raon-l'Etape, a small market town in the Vosges mountains, region of Alsace-Lorraine, near France's western border with Germany. The school had been requisitioned for use as the hospital of the French 315th Army Corps. All over France the military was on the alert, but as yet everything was quiet: it was the period of the 'phony war'. Over the mountains, on the far side of the Rhine, silently stood the massing ranks of Hitler's armies, biding their time.

The policeman, Guillaume Louis, had with him a desperately ill local woman named Rosa Hoffman, wife of Paul Collignon, who earned his living gathering digitalis in the mountain forests. Digitalis – the foxglove plant – is known as 'heartsease' because of its efficacy in treating coronary conditions. Taken in excess it is a poison, though, bringing on rapid and severe vomiting. Unless treated, it can quickly lead to death.

Mme Hoffman had been brought to the hospital from the tiny village of Deyfosses, in Etival, where earlier that day she had received some horrifying news. A detachment from the DST – the French Military Secret Service – had arrested and taken her husband away. Rosa Hoffman's reaction was to try to kill herself. Guillaume Louis handed her over to the chief surgeon, Lieutenant Alain Cuenot, and it is for this reason we are able to relate the tale.

Rosa's husband drove an old Citrôen truck around the mountain roads, but not only in his quest for the foxglove plant: he also stopped regularly, high in the Chipotte Pass, where he would use a radio, supplied by the Nazis, to transmit over the mountains into Germany details of French troop movements. He was one link in a chain that, since 1938, the Nazis had been establishing in the rear of the Maginot line. The purpose of the espionage was, obviously, to keep track of where the French strengths and weaknesses were when the time came to invade (and to confirm to the Germans that the Allies were being as stupid as they suspected). But as Cuenot remembers, another aim was to demoralise the Allied forces:

> Perhaps some Frenchmen remember the extraordinary effect on the morale of the troops when shortly after having eaten poorly cooked beans or having been inspected by a commanding officer, they heard a broadcast from Stuttgart repeating this news in detail. It was all the more astonishing in that the details were sometimes insignificant, very recent, or considered very secret.[3]

Paul Collignon had only been intercepted by chance. From a position so shallow within French territory, it was almost impossible for French Intelligence to pick up transmissions. Unusually (for German technology) Collignon's transceiver had developed a fault. This forced him to telephone a radio repairman in Paris – who was also a German spy and whose 'phone was tapped – and arrange a rendezvous at a café in Nancy to collect a new part. It was on the Place de la Gare, hard by the railway station, and there the French intelligence officers, who had monitored the call, seized the unlucky agents.

While Rosa Hoffman recovered at Cuenot's field hospital, she was questioned by the same men who had arrested her husband. Cuenot recounts that over meals with them in the mess, they told him something about Ernst vom Rath that later, when he wrote his study of the Herschel Grynszpan case, he simply could not bring himself to believe.

CHAPTER ONE

THE EARLY YEARS

Herschel Grynszpan was born on 28 March, 1921, in the city of Hanover, but that was never enough to make him a German citizen. In the eyes of the law his parents were foreign, born in what had been Russia but became Poland after the First World War, and that made Herschel a foreigner, too. It was his special bad luck, though, to be not only Polish but Jewish as well.

With historical hindsight Herschel's multiple misfortunes appear daunting, but the ones that could be seen at the time were bad enough. Life was hard for poor Jewish immigrants then, and soon to grow much grimmer with the advent of the depression at the end of the 'twenties. In the Jewish ghettos of western and central Europe, survival itself was often precarious. Rates of infant mortality were atrocious, nearer late Renaissance levels than those we would recognise as twentieth century.[1]

Added to this were generations of malnutrition and the lowered expectations of poor Jews like the Grynszpans. It bred a certain hardiness of the organism (if a body made it past the bumpy landing of infancy) but along with it a reduced biological optimum. Herschel himself was an undersized child although a feisty one. His body showed signs of a degeneration mapped over many lifetimes of his bloodline. Looking for a different kind of degeneracy, doctors later claimed to have found in Herschel evidence of inherited syphilis (namely his widely spaced and deeply ridged teeth), but it was much more likely an absence of dentistry, together with the generational effects of a protein-poor diet, first farmed in Russia, then eked out in Poland, and lastly scraped together in Germany.

Herschel's parents, Sendel and Ryfka, had emigrated to Hanover in 1911, a year after they were married. Born in Russia, Sendel had served in the Tsar's army (and one of his sons would later fight for the Soviet Red Army against Hitler), and he later travelled west with his pretty young wife to find a better life. As it was, they wound up in the scrofulous and dirt-poor ghetto of the town named after the 'high bank' (Hohe Ufer = Hanover) facing the Leine river.[2] It was also the name of a street in this Jewish or 'Old' quarter, which was a place you could go if you wanted to be mugged with certainty. While the Jews of the quarter kept themselves respectable – and the Grynszpans were orthodox if not particularly religious – that part of town was largely beyond the law and beyond the standard *burgerlich* culture of the gentile Germans.

The police mostly kept out of the ghetto, with the consequence that it developed an underworld, an inverted realm of misrule, where prostitutes, thieves and homosexuals lived together in economic and sexual promiscuity,[3] a last pocket of the old tradition of the medieval outlaw camp, such as London still had in its East End until late Victorian times. It is not surprising that the area became at least partly self-regulating, though still utterly brutal, and in the Scheiber Market even managed a sort of minor economy of second-hand dealers and fences, purveyors of cheap liquor and drugs, scavengers and rentiers of the most depraved and opportunistic sort. It was a dark mirror to the overwhelming and proud conformity of the German bourgeoisie, an upturned slop-bucket of respectable society's subconscious.

When Herschel was a toddler, the homosexual killer Georg Haarmann roamed the streets of this Old quarter, searching for the boys and young men whom he would chop up and sell as tasty morsels in his butcher shop to the good citizens of Hanover. He was a monster beyond doubt, but there is a certain metaphorical perfection to his culinary moonlighting.[4]

Death was an everyday phenomenon in this part of town, and the Grynszpans were not singled out by it for any special treatment. Of Ryfka's eight children, only four made it past infancy, and three past childhood. How many made it to maturity is a question we will address later. During the years this story is concerned with, Herschel's two surviving siblings were Mordechai and Esther (or Marcus and Berta as they were also known, in a touching and practical convention designed to make them appear more German). The Grynszpans were an intelligent and versatile family, despite their little education. Mordechai was a competent and diligent young man who worked as a plumber. Esther earned her living as a secretary. Both still lived at home, but by the standards of the time they were just beginning to pull ahead of the game when the Nazis got to them. Esther, like her mother, never made it out of the clutches of the Hitlerites.

Sendel had not been lucky in his professional life. Job was not his archetype, but on the other hand was not too far away. In the Old Country it is rumoured he had driven a milk cart. Later, he drifted into tailoring (without, it appears, any special training) and rag-dealing. Once in Hanover he tried his hand unsuccessfully at plumbing, then returned to making clothes. He ran his own business for over a decade but the depression put paid to it, and by 1933 he was living on social security, like much of the rest of Germany.[5]

Herschel grew up watching his frail and malarial father suffer the indignities of poverty and unemployment, but also saw him fight tenaciously to keep his family together, amidst dying infants and discouragement from society, with its signs that, even before the advent of the Nazis, read *Juden Unerwünscht* or 'Jews Not Welcome Here'.[6]

From the beginning the Hitlerites were Herschel's problem. He later claimed he was forced to join the Hitler Youth, but this was one of Herschel's many lies (he lied like he acted – on impulse – a zero sum survival technique that came instinctively to him). In fact, he was too young to join by the time he left Germany, and needless to say the brownshirts would never have wanted him. Herschel remembered being kicked and abused by German children in the streets, but by all accounts he could look after himself. He was a natural and enthusiastic fist-fighter – a dreamy but fierce bantam-cock, like John Keats without the literary talent – and from an early age was a Jew who would fight back without hesitation. His nicknames were 'The Little Hun', partly because of his height and partly because of his temper, and 'Maccabee', after the second century BC revolutionary who was martyred because he refused to break the laws of Moses.[7]

It is worthwhile at this point to try to establish what sort of a character Herschel Grynszpan was. Almost all this evidence comes from after the murder of vom Rath. This was when the Nazis had already vilified Herschel not only as the assassin of their great national hero [sic], but as the visible tip of a vast, submerged conspiracy aimed at Germany by world Jewry. It was after the Jews, fearing for their own still caught within Nazi jurisdiction, condemned Herschel. It was after the French, desperately attempting to placate the looming presence in the country next door, disowned the boy. In fact he was only really loved by his family and from afar, by the United States, this affection manifested in the shape of one woman, whom we will meet later on.

There is, needless to say, reams of information on Herschel's personality in the pre-trial documents, and both Cuenot and Schwab make extensive use of it. What must be remembered, though, is that the professionals who were practicing their observations and speculations on Herschel had as their subject a young man at the mercy of two legal systems – one rather hostile and one incandescent with rage at him – and who was incarcerated in a foreign country, the language of which he knew only imperfectly. In other words, for all his bravado Herschel was scared out of his wits: he sounded off more than he otherwise or normally might have done, and was more candid than he should have been. This was a special problem, since he was having to think on his feet all the time, adding complicated fabrications and revisions to a story only extant in his own head. He acted fast to save his life, and actively attempted to cause the Nazis as much trouble as possible – a skill which he later mastered to great effect. And he was also desperately trying, from a position of apparent impotence, to help his pathetically vulnerable family. It is no wonder that contemporary descriptions repeat that Herschel wore the countenance of a hunted animal. If we cannot read confusion and honest cunning as well as fear in his face, and instead simply take all that he revealed as quite normal for him, then we are in danger of misjudging the boy, as others have done before.

The depositions taken from everyone who ever had anything to do with Herschel in Germany were extracted, moreover, by the Gestapo. Bearing in mind their well-documented methods for getting what they wanted out of people, I suggest we treat some of the more extreme criticisms of Herschel with a pinch of salt.

So what was he like? In short he was energetic, temperamental, physically lazy, a big-time fibber, snobbish and aloof, fanatical, a fantasist, and sentimental (and sentimentality has its brutish underside). We can also call him paranoid, as long as its definition includes the possibility that they really are out to get you. He was self-obsessed, but as an egotist he included the entire Jewish people within this obsession. He was sartorially dapper, if not actually vain (the photographs taken after Herschel's arrest make him look like a smooth gangster dude, with his cool raincoat and slicked-back hair), and he liked to flirt with the girls.

Any veteran parent will readily identify this description as an identikit picture of a typical teenager. Anything *less* would be abnormal.

But at the time the world thought differently, and so did Cuenot years after. Schwab's is the more balanced view, but even he discounts the sheer normality I propose was personified in Herschel Grynszpan. It could be argued that he was an ordinary teenager provoked to an extreme act by extraordinary circumstances, but to this there is the objection that others in his position did not do the same, and therefore he is exceptional. It is materially correct to say this, but factually wrong. Firstly, there was an almost identical assassination, by a young Jewish man of a German embassy official, in Switzerland. Comparisons were drawn at the time of Herschel's crime by the Nazis (genuinely paranoid according to the normal definition), who sincerely believed the second murder was conclusive evidence of a Jewish plot. The first occurred three years earlier and transpired as a much more minor incident, for reasons we will examine later. Secondly, others in Herschel's position *did* act similarly, and there are numerous examples of more heroic and suicidal Jewish resistance. But that was largely *after* the victims of Nazism knew what they were up against and had nothing to lose.

Thirdly, I would say that only Herschel acted as he did precisely because he was in a pretty unique position (as opposed to being a unique and even heroic person – although that is what he eventually grew to be). In November 1938 there were about 12,000 Jews in the world who had suffered what one might call 'stage two' Nazi aggression, meaning mistreatment en masse at the hands of official government agencies rather than the attentions of unofficial thugs. Herschel was one of the few people directly connected to their suffering, yet separated from it, and at the same time threatened, as a stateless fugitive, with being returned. Not too many teenagers were condemned like Herschel to the shadows and to living a surreal nocturnal life, and in this respect Herschel was quite unique. Not uniquely fanatical or foolhardy or selfish, but uniquely located and harried, and distraught and angry and unafraid to fight however he could.

Furthermore, although disgraceful Nazi edicts against Jews were being enacted in Germany even by 1936 – like being excluded from the right to an education and a living, and being forced to register all property and possessions preparatory to later sequestration – they remained small beer compared with what was to follow. As for the unleashing of officially sanctioned brutality, the yellow stars, the exclusion from *any* way of earning a living, the mass deportations to concentration camps and the concept of the Final Solution, all this was yet to come.

By virtue of where he was and what he was suffering, and where his family was and what *they* were suffering (and by virtue of the fact that against the odds he found this out by means of a postcard from his sister, Esther), Herschel somehow saw the future more clearly than anyone else on the planet. And he felt its chill at bone zero.

Herschel has been a victim of the *post hoc ergo propter hoc* fallacy, as I shall argue. He was the catalyst for Kristallnacht but not the cause; he encouraged the Nazis to reveal to the world at large their true nature sooner than they would have done. Surely Herschel must be thanked and not blamed for this. Then again, he showed up the complacency of Western nations and their governments, which attracted subtle ignominy towards him from 'respectable' quarters.

Above all, his act constituted a one-man declaration of war, and this is undeniably bad for the status quo. Herschel's act has been called stupid and selfish in that it led directly to the sufferings of thousands of other Jews a couple of days later. But in the face of this, it is Herschel's prescience that must be celebrated. Somewhere in his soul he had stumbled upon a certainty – regardless of all other 'authoritative' claims, Nazi, Jewish and international – that everything was certainly not alright. By the morning he shot vom Rath, Herschel knew at a pre-conscious level that there was already a war being prosecuted: it was a total war in which he and other Jews had nothing certain to gain but certainly nothing to lose by fighting utterly and immediately. It was the old street-fighting instinct of an undersized combatant that told him to hit first and with everything he had. I am certain he was not wrong.

Added to all this must be the aspect of Herschel's character that gets talked about less, but which is profound and touching. We know now from sociology and anthropology the dire effects that extreme poverty and deprivation can have on the family unit. Divorce, abuse and delinquency among poor families disenfranchised by the societies in which they tenuously exist can be disturbingly though not surprisingly high. The Jews are specialists in resisting such erosions of intimacy, and have evolved a tight and loyal (maybe sometimes overbearing and oppressive) family unit, centred around the mother, as a first line of defence. There is no evidence Herschel suffered from a Jewish Mother, though he may have been a little spoiled (he was after all the surviving 'baby' of the family). On the contrary, all the evidence is that he loved his parents and his siblings deeply and abidingly, and that this love was amply returned. Instead of using either personal problems or the harsh environment in which he grew up as a prompt to turn on those close to him, which is a common tactic amongst people whose character is weak, he only chose to cleave more closely to them.

Pity and affection won out over disgust at his father's misfortunes (a rarer achievement than one might suppose), and it is interesting that Herschel originally wanted to be a plumber as his father had been and his brother Mordechai still was. Likewise his father had been a tailor, and we know that Herschel was a snappy dresser, within his humble means, and something of a fashion expert. This too may indicate love and loyalty. There is no evidence of the usual, workaday Oedipal rebellions that enable teenagers to gain a distance from what they see as constricting elders. This may be because Herschel was such a sorry and infantile figure that it did not occur to him, and he was still in a childish, imitative phase; or it may be because he was from the start a serious and independent personality, of the sort destined to become a leader, a mover and shaker, independent and self-reliant but also loving and considerate. And these latter qualities are perfectly cogent with the lethally quick, knife-edge decisions that despatch enemies quickly and decisively,

and with the readiness to retaliate and 'get in the first punch' that
had earned Herschel his childhood nicknames.

What must not be lost sight of, though, is that Herschel annoyed
almost everyone he came into contact with outside his immediate
family. It is clear that his sterling qualities, if such they were, were
still nascent (we shall see them born and grow in the later and even
darker period of his life) and obscured by adolescent uppityness. He
quarrelled most significantly with his relatives in Paris, and was recalcitrant afterwards; he drove his expensive lawyer to distraction,
needled the French jurists, and later on he rendered the Nazis so
apoplectic that the Gestapo seems to have developed a grudging
respect and even an affection for him – a deeply strange phenomenon that will be examined later.

Back in Hanover it was plain from an early age that Herschel had
no time for school. His report cards described him as a poor pupil
and even a disruptive one. After 1933, when he was twelve, he
showed signs of improvement, though. The Nazis claimed that the
apparent rehabilitation dating from then was attributable to their
wholesome influence on German life (Hitler seized power in 1933),
but actually it was just Herschel growing up a little.[8] The Nazis failed
to mention that before Jewish children were excluded from school,
they were forced to sit at the back of the classroom, and that it was
despite and not because of this that Herschel apparently bucked up
his ideas. Herschel lied (again) when he claimed he had graduat-
ed high school. All he received when he was fourteen and old
enough to get the hell out was a certificate of attendance, an
Abgangzeugnis, which did not even prove he was literate[9] – which he
most certainly was, apart from some sentimental clichés and pomposity that showed up in his writings. Cuenot takes Herschel's prose
efforts, such as his prison diary, written under conditions already
described above, as more evidence of his selfish and self-aggran-
dising personality. I would rather suggest, gently, that the prose style
was pretty good for a teenager in the eye of such a storm, and he was
always articulate despite certain infelicities of style – but let that pass.

It cannot be denied that Herschel was held back for several grades several times, and then left education with apparent unconcern for his future. Typical, said the Nazis, not just of this miscreant's whole attitude, but of shiftless and untrustworthy Jewry as a whole. But if looked at another way, Herschel's behaviour was smart, responsible and eminently sane. For example, if you are banished to the back of class by your government you might rationalise that, if you are obviously unwanted, what you are being taught might not be much use to you. You might in fact leave as soon as possible in order to pursue a better education and a better future elsewhere. And this is exactly what Herschel did.

CHAPTER TWO

SCHOOL'S OUT

When Herschel was not being a lazy good-for-nothing at school, as the Nazis claimed, he was attending the local synagogue with great regularity and exhibiting exemplary behaviour. Herschel at fourteen was passionately religious. Partly this was because his Jewish identity was daily being reconfirmed for him by the Germans, whether he liked it or not. Anti-semitic posters were plastered over the shopfront of his father's small tailor shop, and he was being kicked even by young children, he claimed, at least twice a day.[1] Partly, though, his religious dedication may have been a fallout from the hormonal changes of adolescence. Herschel was denied an outlet for sexual energy in at least two ways: firstly by the orthodoxy of his family's religious observations, and secondly by the fact that he was undersized and immature in appearance, not to mention flat broke. Herschel may have become passionate about the Old Testament as a way of dealing with the surges of energy to which a teenager is subject. There was also the simple fact that religion supplied him with a rich, complete world, a sense of belonging, and a morally interrogative way of interpreting the deeply strange circumstances in which (this being

Hitler's Germany in 1935) he found himself. It was his sea anchor and a true love, but it was an immersion that touched on the hinterlands of fanaticism, and this aspect I propose was certainly underpinned by sexual frustration.

But Herschel was never fanatical to any inhuman degree, and as we have seen, there were good practical reasons for his enthusiasm. It is vital to say that here, because Herschel did go on to commit what was arguably a fanatical crime. But his religious adherence is also more evidence that he was not the sly and idle sub-criminal the Nazis tried to make him seem. Duplicity was not beyond him, but as we shall see there were from early on extenuating circumstances surrounding his lies and self-deceptions.

Herschel's attempts to find work after he had quit school were brief and half-hearted. Schwab[2] reiterates Cuenot's estimation of Herschel's worth in the job-market and it was not good[3]. He was a dreamy boy, an apprentice *flaneur,* as the French has it. He liked tinkering with things mechanical but never seriously applied himself to technics. In general he was being a teenager in a difficult and complex world, processing a lot of troubling information regarding his future. As this meant going for many long walks, commentators have assumed it was laziness. Being orthodox meant that he would not work on Saturdays (which has also been uncharitably interpreted as sloth) and this did not help his chances of finding a job either.

More to the point, though, was the fact that Jews were increasingly being excluded from economic activity. This worked right down the line: Sendel, the father, was receiving fewer customers. Non-Nazi Germans, of whom there were naturally many, faced pressure from brown-shirted thugs if they patronised Jewish businesses. Mordechai and Esther were paid less than gentiles for their work by now, and promotion was effectively denied. These informal constraints were soon to be made official, and the future was pretty clear even then. The whole family knew this, and was already making plans to send Herschel, as the youngest, away where he would have

more of a chance at life. He was their hope. Schwab says Herschel
was criticised for not finding work (he does not tell us by whom),
but that the situation under which the family lived would have discouraged the ambitions of the most determined job-seeker, 'And
Herschel was not such an individual'[4]. Well, this last point is debat-
able. Herschel did have plans, and before his period of
unemployment, he enrolled at a Jewish Talmudic school, a
'Yeshiva' in Frankfurt-am-Main, and remained there for one year. He
was sent there by the 'Miraschi', a Zionist group Sendel had
Herschel join as soon as he left school. The master-plan formulated by his family was for Herschel to emigrate to Palestine, the
'Promised Land'. The Miraschi actually paid for him to attend
Yeshiva, where Herschel studied Hebrew and related subjects. The
college was designed to prepare young Jews for the spiritual pro-
fessions, and the teaching was way above Herschel's head. But it was
to teach him also what the Zionists regarded as essential intellectual
and cultural kit for a new immigrant to their lands in the Middle-
East; and this he was capable of acquiring.

The full course of study was supposed to last five years, but
Herschel attended only the freshman period. This was not, as
Schwab implies,[5] necessarily an early, possibly disgraced or lack-
adaisical exit. More likely, he had satisfied the minimum
requirements of the Miraschi for emigration to Palestine. Again, it
is suggestive not of disinterest but of eagerness on Herschel's part:
he really wanted to get out of Germany. His teachers at the Yeshiva
rated Herschel as utterly average, and he committed no infractions
of rules or protocol that stood out in their memories.[6]

However, disappointment awaited Herschel on his return to
Hanover from Frankfurt in April 1936. Palestine was by no means
a safe or easy place to live. It was still being, quite literally, built from
the ground up, and conditions were hard. The Miraschi had sent
Herschel away for a year, saying goodbye to a boy and hoping to welcome back a young man whom they could put on the boat knowing
he would be able to pull his weight. What they got was a Herschel

with better Yiddish and Scripture, but still the body of a twelve year-old. The settlers in Palestine simply could not afford to carry any dead weight, which is what Herschel looked like to the selection board, so he was told to wait one more year. Thus began the period of unemployment, and a re-drawing of plans, albeit temporary, to fill the time before he would leave Europe for the Holy Lands.

The situation was growing worse at home. The Nazi governmental machine, busily collapsing the separation of powers between legislature, judiciary and executive essential for justice and democracy, had begun publishing its truly diabolical Nuremburg Decrees. The first came on September 15, 1935, which included an anti-miscegenation law (Jews were now no longer allowed to marry or even have sexual relationships outside their 'race'); an edict stripping all Jews, not just 'foreign' ones like Herschel, of their German citizenship – they were now mere guests, and unwelcome ones at that; and some strange, sexually obsessive laws, such as not allowing Jews to employ as servants young Aryan females.[7]

Later, during the period of real genocide, Jews were transformed into 'vermin' in the Nazi mind, partly by the repetition of the word through previous years: this made it easier to kill them, for such is the power of language. But before then the Jews seem to have undergone a sort of sexual demonisation, part of a larger metaphor the Nazis were deploying which concerned the 'rape' and (sexual) infection of pure and wholesome Germany by the underhand and licentious semites. It sounds absurd but it is recognisably a more hysterical version of white fears about blacks. What is more, the Nazis were absolutely sincere in their beliefs: witness the po-faced and nit-picking fashion in which they carried out their arbitrary laws even when they could have done, in reality, whatever they liked. This is worth saying now, because it will help to explain the odd behaviour of the Nazis later on, when Herschel was in their hands but they still insisted on doing everything by the book, down to the last comma and period point. It was one of the contradictions of the Nazi mind that Herschel learned expertly to exploit.

Later, in mid-November of 1935, another set of decrees was issued out of Nuremburg, and this one cost Esther and Mordechai Grynszpan their jobs. Jews were no longer allowed to earn a living. The desire for Herschel to go abroad had quickly become a necessity, since it would now be difficult for the Grynszpans even to feed themselves (all this as early as 1935, remember). During his later cross-examination by the medical and legal experts, Herschel recalled what had propelled him on the next leg of his unlucky journey through the Europe of the 1930s:

> One day at the synagogue I met an old man who said that it was difficult to find a boy like me who studied the books. He asked me to come to visit him. It was old Katz, the watchmaker. But I don't like to talk with men whom I don't know. However, I accepted the old man's invitation. He advised me not to stay in Germany. He said to me, 'A boy like you can't stay here under such conditions. In Germany a Jew is not a man, but is treated like a dog.' I told him that all the governments were closed to me [sic]. He advised me to go to France.[8]

Katz the watchmaker was not just a wise old man, but also a kind and considerate one. He took it upon himself to talk to Herschel's father about the eminently sensible strategy of sending the boy elsewhere in Europe, at least until Herschel had filled out enough to swing a pickaxe in Palestine, and Sendel concurred enthusiastically. France was the destination of preference for Herschel, but there were insurmountable complications.

In the broadest sense, the Nuremburg decrees concocted by Hitler and his cohorts were having the desired effect. Until around 1939, the aim of the Nazis was forcibly to encourage the Jews to leave German territory. Herschel and at least 200,000 others took the hint, and this one third of German Jewry had left by the outbreak of the Second World War (though most thereafter rapidly found to their dismay that they were once again within German jurisdiction).

As life grew increasingly poisonous for Jews inside the Third Reich, the democratic countries were unreserved in their sympathy for the plight of these poor people. However, that sympathy did not extend to a relaxation of immigration controls. The most verbally supportive governments – those of France, Great Britain, the USA and Poland – were also the ones whose rules were tightened to prevent an influx of refugees from the Nazis. Perhaps in political terms this is the price of verbal support. At any rate, the free world was staring with horror at a re-tooling and re-arming Germany, aggressive in its attitude (for example, General Motors had plant within the Reich that it was forced to switch to Nazi war production purposes on pain of sequestration: General Motors did as it was told), and had decided to put up the shutters and ignore what was coming.

The chief bureaucratic absurdity confronting Herschel in his desire to relocate to France was that the Nazis would not allow him to leave with any assets, although they were otherwise keen for him to go. Herschel was simply not allowed to take money out when he went. France, on the other hand, was not interested in letting in anyone who was bereft of visible means of support, despite the fact that the Grynszpans had relatives settled in the country.[9] There was a way around this, however. Belgium was not so strict (smaller countries being often the kinder), and would allow Herschel in on certain conditions.

Sendel had four brothers: Isaac, Wolf, Salomon and Abraham. These were liberally distributed through Europe, and luckily Wolf was living in Brussels, thus satisfying the Belgian government's primary requirement for Herschel to enter their country. In Belgium it was possible to apply to the French Consulate for a visa that would allow entry to France. The only condition to be satisfied on that score was the price of admission, a modest 50 francs. It appeared the fix was in.

It should be said that Herschel left Hanover to embark on his sad odyssey in July 1936, a mere ten weeks after he had left the Yeshiva. That means if he was a willing layabout, he was not willing for very long, but rather decided to act and alter the course of his life. In

mid-July, before he left Germany, Herschel went to stay for a fortnight with his uncle Isaac in the industrial town of Essen. It is not
clear why he went. There is no apparent reason for the visit, but
there are a couple of possible ones. Firstly, Isaac could have been
invoked to dispense words of wisdom to the youth. Fathers often
find that an uncle can be an oracle to a teenager, while they themselves are listened to only with reluctance. Secondly, Herschel's trip
to Essen (a strange place for a vacation) might have been more evidence of his generous and affectionate nature. Uncle Isaac and his
family were the only other close relatives in Germany, and
Herschel had gone to say farewell to them. He may have feared for
them as well as his own family, after all. Once more, such actions on
his part argue against the descriptions of Herschel as selfish, egotistical and unthinking.

Herschel arrived in Brussels at the end of July 1936, travelling on
a Polish passport since he was never entitled to a German one. At
this point his papers were in order as far as both the German and
Belgian governments were concerned – but even so, for the reader
the technicalities of inter-war bureaucracy as they apply here are
bewildering, and we shall simplify as much as possible.

Just before Herschel left for his farewell visit with Uncle Isaac, he
had applied for a German exit visa. This tells us that Herschel's mind
was made up to go before he travelled to Essen, so whatever Isaac
was possibly going to advise his nephew on, emigration was not it.
Herschel already had in his back-pocket the Polish passport he had
obtained from its consulate, now stamped with the exit visa. It
allowed him to return to Germany and his family on or before 1
April 1937. This gave Herschel nearly a year abroad to prepare for
Palestine.[10] He was ready to go.

On his return from Essen, Herschel stayed with his family only
long enough to pack a bag before catching an international train
to Brussels. He bade farewell to his parents, Sendel and Ryfka, to his
sister Esther and brother Mordechai, with sadness but with no earth-
ly idea that this would be the last time he would ever see them again.

A day or two later, at the end of July, he arrived in Brussels, and experienced his first real let-down.

Uncle Wolf Grynszpan and his wife, Lea, lived at 37 rue des Tanneries in the Belgian capital. Like Sendel, Wolf was a tailor, and also like Sendel, he was quite poor and living an almost hand-to-mouth existence. At least this is Herschel's disarming explanation for the coolness with which he was received:

> Due to the ban on export capital, it was impossible for me to take more than 10 marks so that I had almost no money with me upon arrival in Brussels. [Uncle Wolf and aunt Lea] welcomed me rather coldly because I arrived with no funds and my sojourn imposed additional expense upon them.[11]

It should be stressed again here that there is nothing melodramatic or self-pitying in Herschel's words, none of the egocentric teenage whining so much commentary would lead us to expect. And there should be, really: here is a mere boy, abroad for the first time and beset with anxiety not only on his own account but also on that of his family. He arrives expecting to find warmth and affection in the arms of close family, but is rejected. Herschel's eminently practical and mature response is not to throw up his hands in despair or sink into self-pity, but simply to acknowledge the situation, provide a satisfactory reason for it, and then to go and stay with a neighbour, Zaslawsky (apparently a distant relative), who lived two doors away at number 33, and did not mind a little company and an extra place at the dinner-table. Zaslawsky also informed Herschel in no uncertain terms that he was not to outstay his welcome, and like a bright and mature young man, Herschel made the best of the situation. We can imagine, though, that for the highly strung and lonely Herschel this was a trying and unhappy period.

He only stayed six weeks in Belgium, and such brevity attests to the chilly welcome that awaited him. But it also shows something else. From his unhappy sojourn in Brussels can be detected

Herschel's longer-range intentions, and I believe these did not originally include domicile in France, though it seems to have been
assumed this was so. For example, his planned emigration to
Palestine later becomes discounted as a cover story for his real aim.
Cuenot basically discards the Palestinian dream because he is so convinced of Herschel's lazy and shiftless nature. He implies it would
be out of character for the boy seriously to have desired a hard and
strenuous start-over on another continent, given his aversion to
physical labour. He thinks Herschel was merely trawling around,
attempting to net the fattest fish to feed him. The Nazis, obsessive-
ly attempting to prove the Jewish conspiracy, had Herschel
planning assassination and sabotage all along. For them, he was
already set on his course to destroy vom Rath when still living in
Hanover.

What nobody takes into account is uncle Wolf's coldness to
Herschel and the reason for it. I think the blindingly obvious explanation is that Wolf thought he was getting Herschel for good. Like
Isaac, he was pleased to have his nephew visit for a couple of weeks,
but found imposed fatherhood at that time of his life too much to
bear, quite apart from the expense. Also, like Sendel, the kind of business he was in, supplying a few dresses to local department stores, was
not the kind of venture that could be readily expanded to take on an
unskilled apprentice. Herschel spoke little French and of course no
Flemish, and probably would not have been eligible for a work permit anyway, so for all intents and purposes he was only a drain on the
little resources at Wolf and Lea's disposal.

We may censure these unhelpful relatives, but there was little
framework of social help back then, and no clear idea of what
Herschel was going to do to help support himself. There is no evidence that Wolf and Lea had even met Herschel before, so the
emotional ties were not as strong as one might immediately imagine.
Travel for the poor across borders (apart from necessary emigrations) was a luxury that could rarely be indulged, and who knows,
Herschel might have looked to them like he was the pampered young

princeling foisted on them by rich German relatives. There is a suggestion that Wolf was aghast when Herschel arrived penniless – it was not what he was expecting at all – and he may well have supposed Sendel was going to put him on some sort of wages for looking after the nephew. Stop awhile but do not grow too comfortable, was his message on short reflection, and the relatives must not be judged over-harshly because of it, as Herschel considerately realised.

From these circumstances, then, we can readily see that when he arrived in Brussels it was not Herschel's plan to travel illegally over the border to France. He had probably not even thought about Paris at this time, because he was taking each day as it came in a whirlwind of upset, both geographical and emotional. It is likely that long-range planning was not Herschel's specialist subject, and this accords perfectly with the nature and circumstances of the crime he later committed. What is more, if he was not deliberately planning his flight to France then it makes his subsequent action – which directly opened onto Herschel's tragedy – the more poignant for being prompted out of selflessness and concern for his Belgian relatives. He was trying to get out of their way and got in his own way as a result.

It happened as follows. As soon as the situation in Brussels was apparent, there was a flurry of communications between Herschel and his father, then between Sendel and his third brother, Abraham, who lived in Paris. Herschel told his father he could not long remain in Brussels, and Sendel wrote Abraham pleading that he put the poor boy up for a while. Anything to keep him out of the insane hellhole that was Germany. We do not have these letters, but it is a matter of logic to understand what happened, especially considering the brief time during which everything was arranged.

Abraham, like his biblical namesake, was an excellent man, and nobody has a bad word to say about him. Later, when he found himself in prison because of Herschel, he never uttered a word of criticism against his troublesome nephew, and was entirely supportive of him throughout the long pre-trial period. He was a silent, even gruff man, and not one to make a show of his emotions. As is the way of things, this seems to suggest his deeper feelings were generous and abiding. He and his wife, Chawa, had not been blessed with children. Like Wolf and Lea it appears that, apart from the Hanover Grynszpans, the family were not great breeders. Also like Wolf and Lea, Abraham and Chawa were poorly off; but unlike them, the middle-aged couple leaped at the chance of an instant family, and were impatient to greet Herschel with open arms.

In the event, Abraham went to the length of legally adopting Herschel as his own son, and a document acknowledging this was issued on 19 October, 1936.[12] This was a mere three weeks after Herschel arrived in Paris, so the process of transferring guardianship of Herschel must have been set in train earlier – possibly a mere week or so after he arrived in Brussels, since that is the length of time it would have taken for Herschel to write to his father, and his father to contact Abraham. It would roughly accord with the date of the new paternity arrangements. It also shows the family's desperation to keep Herschel out of Hitler's way. Again, he was plainly a well-loved boy. And again, this argues more for bungling than premeditation on Herschel's part as far as illegally entering France was concerned. Perhaps Sendel and Abraham even thought that if Herschel was the latter's adopted son, it would allow him to stay in France. If so, then they thought wrong.

Zaslawsky, with whom Herschel was boarding, had a sister who lived in Paris, Mme Rosenthal. In September 1936 she had been vacationing in Ostend, and swung by to visit her brother before she returned to France. She arrived at 33 rue des Tanneries at an opportune time, and was prevailed on to help Herschel slip across the border into France, which he did on 16 September. As Cuenot describes it, this was a very simple operation.[13] There was tight bureaucracy keeping the European populations separate, but the physical controls were looser. France and Belgium, politically, culturally and linguistically so close, even forewent the usual border formalities in certain cases, and many workers living in Belgium travelled across into the neighbouring country to their places of employment, and vice-versa. This gave Herschel his chance. If he could slip through during the morning rush hour then he would be home free. Why then did he need Zaslawsky's sister to help him? Probably because he would look like her son, and thus not arouse suspicion. If she were asked for her passport, the guards would probably be satisfied and not ask to see Herschel's. What is more, she could do the talking. Herschel later learned to get by quite well speaking French, but at this date he was obviously German, and that would have meant trouble. He looked younger than he was, and the guards would naturally address only his 'mother'.

To travel across the border, from Quievrain in Belgium to Valenciennes was thus an easy manœuvre. As Cuenot says that travellers with no baggage were hardly ever checked, since it looked like they were on their way to work, he implies Herschel left his valise behind. I think he was more daring and took it along. Mme Rosenthal would have been carrying luggage home from her holiday anyway, so there was a valid explanation. In any event they were not questioned, and were met on the French side by an eager Uncle Abraham who had arrived by train from Paris to greet his new 'son'. Herschel later denied Abraham had been there, in order to try and save his uncle from more severe punishment. Once more we can see that not all his lies were self-serving.

The interesting question, since the rest of the story really stems from this needlessly illegal entry into France, is why on earth did not Herschel simply purchase a visa? It was only 50 francs, after all.

There could be many reasons. For a start, Herschel was probably feeling somewhat paranoid by this stage, and preferred to have no contact with governmental authorities. It could also have been (which is mentioned by neither Cuenot or Schwab) that the validity of Herschel's German exit visa, which allowed him into Belgium in the first place, was dependent on him remaining there to study in preparation for his emigration to Palestine. Perhaps he thought that by getting a French visa, he was invalidating his other rights –

and he may even have been correct, given the abrasiveness of the German authorities. To have been officially in France may have signified in Herschel's troubled young mind that he would not be able to see his family again. Perhaps he was discouraged by now and was thinking of returning to Hanover, seeing Paris only as a stopover and keeping quiet about it because he knew his family wanted him to stay out of Germany. Perhaps he simply worried that the French, refusing him entry at the German border, might also turn him away at the Belgian.

What is certain is that Wolf would not give Herschel the necessary 50 francs. Neither did his father, but that is understandable, because it was extremely difficult to transfer money out of Germany. That Abraham (not rich, but generous) did not send the money argues that the decision to slip across the border was a spontaneous one, maybe sparked by Mme Rosenthal's arrival at Zaslawsky's house. Perhaps alternatively everybody thought that since getting into France was so easy, why waste good money on a visa? If Herschel was going to be Abraham's legal ward, then by the time the French found out about his residence it would be a *fait accompli* – Herschel would be practically a French citizen.

The last possibility is that Herschel lied and told everyone his passport was good for France. Yet from the little already established of Herschel's character, I find this hard to believe. He later insisted on the ignorance of all those involved to save them from trouble as best he could. But if they really were ignorant, why the elaborate subterfuge at the border?

It doubtless seemed a minor transgression at the time, but given the murderous intentions of the Nazis, and an uncaring world, it was the beginning of disaster for Herschel.

CHAPTER THREE

LIFE IN PARIS

Two people's fates were to conflict violently in Paris, and we have not yet encountered the second, the victim of Herschel's crime, a young German diplomat named Baron Ernst vom Rath. He was the innocent and unwilling participant in this tragedy, claimed as a martyr by the Hitlerites, and denounced by Herschel's supporters as a Nazi perpetrator who deserved what he got. Vom Rath, then, was posthumously insulted twice over: firstly by Hitler and his cohorts using him for propaganda purposes, and secondly by Herschel's defence (and later Herschel himself) who accused the Baron of homosexuality – he was supposedly Herschel's tormentor and seducer. His father and brother were forced into the public eye and made to stand for ideas with which they were uncomfortable, and in later years had to defend Ernst's name in the courts against sexual and financial libels.[1]

My contention in this book is that the crux of the personal tragedy lies in the fact that Herschel 'chose' as his victim possibly the one German in existence whom he should not have shot, and that vom Rath had a very different and secret identity to those claimed by either the defence or the prosecution before the trial. There is some hard evidence for what I will argue, and other merely circumstantial. Part of what I say, though, will of necessity be speculation.

It is important before Herschel's next experiences make us inevitably sympathise too deeply with him, that we attempt to draw a firm outline of the young Baron's life and character. As I believe he was innocent of the disgraces being enacted by the Nazi fanatics – perhaps more than innocent – I want to persuade the reader to like vom Rath at the outset: if not then the danger is he will be tarred by the same brush we justifiably use on the Nazis. Vom Rath is a special case, and my argument is that the damage Herschel did with his crime was not to spark Kristallnacht, (Schwab agrees there was a positive net effect for German and Austrian Jewry) but instead to cut the head off a force for the good in Hitler's Germany.

The vom Raths were an old German family, and as the prefix suggests, of the upper class. Ernst's father had been a government lawyer, and later had become an industrialist, leaving the civil service to run the family's sugar factory.[2] He had three sons of whom Ernst was the oldest, and also a daughter who died in infancy. Like his father, Ernst studied law, becoming an apprentice magistrate in Königsberg in 1932 when he was 21 years old. He later moved to Berlin, where he continued to work at the same job for a short while before he came to the decision to enter the diplomatic service. He began at the Foreign Ministry in Berlin in 1934, helped along no doubt because his uncle Roland Koester was at the time German ambassador to France. He worked hard and passed his probation and exams, practising for the language finals by spending the summer of that year in Paris. In the spring of 1935 he was back there as an attaché and then as his uncle's personal assistant. Incidentally, his uncle Roland also ran the intelligence desk.

Vom Rath continued working in Paris until his uncle died almost a year later. What is interesting is that he was then immediately reassigned to Berlin (he would have preferred to remain in France performing his very pleasant job), and this suggests that it was Roland's influence rather than any popularity of Ernst himself within the service that had obtained him his sought-after position. I should repeat: by this time the Nazis were running the show, even making inroads into the conservative and rather anti-Nazi Foreign Ministry, and vom Rath apparently had no high-up friends there. This is more than confirmed by his next posting, which was to Calcutta, a place whose inhabitants the Nazis would regard as sub-human. It was also bad luck for the delicate diplomat, who came down with what appears to have been amœbic dysentery. (Incidentally, while in India, both before and during his fever, it was reported that he was very free in his criticisms of the Nazi regime: this may have been resentment at his treatment or it may have been, as I suspect, evidence of something deeper. Later on in Europe he was mute where his opinions were concerned, and there may have been good reasons for this.) He had to be evacuated to Germany. He was also diagnosed as suffering from pulmonary tuberculosis, and spent months recovering at a sanatorium in the Black Forest.

Vom Rath was not a well man. It was the middle of 1938 before he was re-posted (and promoted to head of cultural affairs) to Paris – happiness for this sensitive francophile – and he was promoted again in October to the position of Secretary of Legation (*Legationsskretär*). After all his bad luck and illness, vom Rath was at last where he wanted to be. But less than a month later he was dead by an assassin's bullet, and his body was in Berlin, draped in a Nazi flag, with a curiously disapproving Hitler himself in the funeral congregation. Vom Rath through no fault, design or wish of his own, had become the first great Nazi martyr, and (after Horst Wessel) its original war hero, the cause for revenge which led to Kristallnacht and the acceleration of the persecution of the Jews. Not long after, when Poland refused to accept the refugees Germany was sending it, and sent back to Hitler his Polish Germans into the bargain, the führer invaded and the Second World War began.

It has been asserted in vom Rath's defence by both Cuenot and Schwab that he was a very 'lukewarm' Nazi. But why even say this? There is nothing in the brief biography above to suggest that vom Rath was a Nazi at all – quite the opposite, in fact. And yet it must be admitted that there is a picture of him, kneeling, smiling in the front row of what is rather like a soccer photograph – except all the of the team are brownshirts, members of the SA, (*Sturmabteilung*) stormtroopers of the NSDAP, the Nazi party. And on vom Rath's arm is the swastika.

He had joined the party way back, before Hitler had become Chancellor, while studying at Königsberg. The university at the outset of the 1930s was a place of intense nationalism, and many young, idealistic and intelligent men had joined along with him. Remember that Germany was in the grip of a terrible depression, partly brought about by the punitive and long-lasting measures of the Treaty of Versailles, imposed by the Allies (against US President Woodrow Wilson's better judgment) at the end of the First World War. Young Germans saw their country being ground into the dust without mercy, and it was natural for them to find such an expression for their concern.

National Socialism, when it first arrived, appeared a noble and patriotic flag around which to rally. It had yet taken on none of the hues of fanaticism and militarism that later came to characterise it, and little of the overt anti-semitism either. During this time, studying at the university, vom Rath apparently had a Jewish girlfriend, and there is no sign he had to hide the fact. At this point Nazism was most concerned with criticising the international banking system that was keeping Germany on its knees. Only later would finance and usury openly become a Jewish conspiracy to the Nazi mind. Hitler at this stage was wisely keeping his own counsel, and rabble-rousing in more general terms.

The other side was the communists, which vom Rath did not join. Partly this was due to his social position (his family was traditional and monarchist), partly because he wanted to have a career, and mostly because to the Germans, the Soviets (like the Russians of the Tsarist empire before them) appeared a threat that is difficult for others in the West to understand, even after the experience of the Cold War. A still greater imperative than the extermination of the Jews to Hitler, from earliest times until the very end of his tyranny, was the threat from the East. His concerns about the Russians led to the mistake of the Eastern campaign, which opened up a second front and led to the Nazis losing the war. Before that, the führer was obsessed with *lebensraum* or 'living space' for the German people that would insulate them from the barbaric hordes (as Hitler saw it) in the East. If there were many more Nazis than communists in Germany during the 1930s, all this must be taken into account. When the Nazis first appeared it was easy for an eager, thrusting and essentially good-hearted young German to see them as the sensible middle way, and a force that could argue internationally for the rights of Germany – something that the old men of the Weimar Republic seemed incapable of doing.

Vom Rath signed up for the NSDAP in the summer of 1932[3], when it was headed by Ernst Röhm, and tensions were already developing between his band of brownshirts (it was a very clubby and cliquey outfit, and this atmosphere was encouraged by the homosexual Röhm), and the more scheming and ambitious Hitler, who had at his disposal Himmler and his 'boys', the *Schutzaffeln* (SS). The tension culminated in what has become known as 'The Night of the Long Knives', when the SS slaughtered most of the top SA brownshirts in their headquarters, killing Röhm and revealing for the first time the true extent of Hitler's capacity for ruthless violence.

Vom Rath grew rapidly disenchanted from this point on, but it was extremely difficult by now to resign. It was undeniably a mistake to have joined the SA, but at least nominal membership of the up-and-coming political movement would not stall vom Rath's career. Had he quit, not only would he have been professionally stymied, but questions would have been asked, and who knows where he would have ended. Cuenot is emphatic on this point, and sums things up well, as follows:

It was at that point [4 July, 1934, Night of the Long Knives] that Hitler for the first time revealed his true self to the German people. He no longer sought to convince and lead by persuasion, but began to attack and to impose himself by force. Without daring to express themselves, without being able to show their fears, the average German, beginning that day, asked himself if the 'Leader' was not mad, or a liar, or an assassin. The police, a network of informants, concentration camps, and executions without trial awaited the fainthearted. It became implausible for anyone to do anything but to submit to the oppression. The 'occupation', which Europe later experienced, was something to which the Germans were subject as of 1934.[4]

He is over-egging the custard just a little, though. There was plenty of popular enthusiasm for Hitler, and a natural seed-bed of resentful petit-bourgeois sentiment against the upper classes, the Jews and the dominating foreigners. Hitler had an unsurpassed genius for appealing to the chauvinism and frustrations of the lower classes and small businessmen.[5] Also, it was not the fainthearted who faced unlawful execution, but the bravehearted who stood up to the thuggery and intimidation. In vom Rath's case I think that, reading between the lines, he was much more than merely disenchanted, and being a Christian,[6] set about doing what he could against the Nazis, as persecution of the Jews and aggressive re-arming began in earnest.

Working in Paris, vom Rath placed himself at a tolerable distance from the goings-on in Germany (the diplomatic service being, as has been noted, no furnace or forge of Nazism) and actively attempted to Frenchify himself, continuing to take lessons in the language from Mlle Taulin, with whom he had first studied during his probationary period in 1934. She had nothing but good to say about him to the pre-trial investigators, remarking especially on his kindness and politeness. She confirmed that while living in Paris he kept himself largely to himself, as his maid, Mlle Ebeling, also affirmed.

Ill-health mostly kept him in at nights, and he did not socialise keenly.[7]

According to Cuenot, however, vom Rath did have one very close and intimate friend to whom he may have been introduced by his uncle. This man was a German, and also one who was by now much happier living outside Germany. His name was Maître von Bose, a jurist who specialised in German law, and whose position as counsellor to the German embassy often sent him there. He was much older than vom Rath and was married to a French woman. This couple may well have been surrogate parents for the otherwise solitary young diplomat, who often dined at their house, and spent long evenings in conversation with von Bose. What else is known of von Bose is as follows: he was cultured and extremely well-connected within French governmental circles – a sort of Peter Ustinov figure – with close and extensive contacts in the *Deuxième Bureaux,* the French Ministry of Intelligence, equivalent to MI6 or the CIA. We know nothing else except that he was treated like a hero by the French government after the end of the Second World War (he died in 1957). I submit that is enough to go on for now.

I hope it is clear from the preceding pages that Herschel in his desperation attacked a man who could only have represented the oppression the Jews were suffering in a symbolic sense. It makes the violence all the more mournful, but the true tragedy will be revealed later, when we expand on what has been hinted at above.

So when Herschel arrived in Paris from Belgium in late September 1936, Ernst vom Rath was occupied contracting life-threatening diseases in Calcutta. He would not return to France until the late summer of 1938, and this is important to stress because it almost certainly proves that he and Herschel had no prior contact before the violent meeting of 8 November that year. Indeed, throughout 1938 Herschel was preoccupied with eluding all sorts of officialdom, for reasons we shall discover below.

Almost the first thing uncle Abraham did when Herschel came to stay was to walk down to the local police station and tell them his nephew was now living with him. This was the first step in a long and fruitless endeavour to obtain for Herschel a resident's permit. The gendarmerie greeted Abraham with a fine for 100 francs, imposed for allowing the boy to enter the country without the visa discussed above. As this fine was twice the cost of the visa itself, it more strongly underlines the argument that the decision to leave Brussels was hurried, and that the visa requirement was seen by the family as an unnecessary delay. It was also, doubtless, part of the attempt to turn Herschel's residence in Paris into a *fait accompli*, as we mentioned above.

By the time he arrived in Paris, Herschel was showing the strains of his short but sharp diaspora. He was a sickly child to begin with, undersized and delicate, the victim of a mild version of rickets in childhood,[8] and apt to worry about life. This showed up chiefly in terrible stomach pains, which is not uncommon in thoughtful, sensitive teenagers. Fretting leads to spasms in the digestive tract, and the kind of crippling indigestion that can double a body up for hours or even days at a time. The best cure is to stop worrying and wait until you grow up, and the next best is plenty of rest and an innocuous diet, which he was promptly placed on. But the plain fact was that Herschel, understandably, was worn out and deeply upset over his recent experiences. He was concerned for his family in Hanover, and missing them terribly. Abraham and Chawa immediately tried to make their charge feel at home at 'Maison Albert', their tiny flat at 23 Boulevard Richard Lenoir, and even went to the extent of moving (to 8 rue Martel) so Herschel would no longer have to sleep in the living room.[9] It was a little more costly, but the middle-aged couple were at last a full-fledged family. Herschel was soon helping around the house and shopping for his aunt, pleased at least to be living in a similar community to the one he had left behind in Germany – predominantly Jewish, with German and Yiddish widely spoken.[10] Even so, he remained solitary to begin with, and it took him a while before his inquisitive and intelligent personality reasserted itself, and led Herschel to develop something of a social life, and an interest in politics and current affairs.

The Yiddish newspapers were not at all parochial, though obviously they carried much news of interest to Jewish people, and Herschel in particular, who followed anti-semitic developments in Germany and elsewhere with a horrified fascination. He also kept abreast of the news in French papers such as *La Journée Parisienne*.[11] I suggest we should not form any opinion of Herschel as an obsessive loner. He had some friends with whom he would go dancing (Herschel claimed he could not dance, but even so he was happy to hang out), to the movies, or on outings to the country. He used to meet his pals outside a café called *Tout Va Bien* (which the Nazis later attempted to make out was a gay bar in order to discredit Herschel's crime as a political statement, until they saw how such a claim might backfire on them), and he belonged to a Polish-Jewish sports club, *L'Aurore*, that organised activities for the youngsters of the district.

In many ways, then, Herschel's lot was not such a bad one. Cuenot is again censorious, seeing Herschel's period of adjustment to his new surroundings, and his precarious status an an illegal alien, as more evidence that the boy was workshy, and developed an image of himself as the persecuted Jewish martyr as a cover for his 'mediocrity'. I cannot agree with this. Besides, Cuenot contradicts himself within the space of a few pages, on the one hand claiming that it 'was not the uncertainty of the period alone which can be blamed for [Herschel's] natural tendency towards laziness',[12] while on the other saying that Herschel 'had a pronounced preference for manual labour'.[13] The boy himself was able to supply a perfectly reasonable explanation for his 'idleness', as he later told the examining magistrate: 'I could have found work if I'd wanted, but I didn't want to put myself in an illegal situation.'

The short answer to this is that he was in an illegal situation anyway, so why not be hung for a sheep instead of a lamb? It is probable, though, that his aunt and uncle (for whom he worked very hard and tried to help as much as possible, so no hint of laziness there) asked him not to get a job. They knew better than anyone that it was best for Herschel to be as invisible as possible, and not to provoke the French authorities. They also simply adored having him around and probably wanted to baby him. It is difficult to imagine Herschel objecting to that kind of affectionate indulgence, given his lonesome situation. Throughout his time in Paris Herschel continued to attend synagogue regularly, and kept up with his study of the Torah. Cuenot speculates that all this intellectual stuff was a pose, an affectation, or that Herschel went about it by rote, like mumbling his beads: cats' cradles to keep the darkness at bay.[14] That sounds patronising, though. Herschel was a bright and streetwise youth, with an interest in history and politics way above the average, and who was, if not gifted, at least sincere in all his activities and interests. I think he used his time most intelligently and productively, sorting his head out and keeping himself from tipping over into sullenness and self-pity. That kind of effort, given his circumstances, takes a lot of mental energy and application: you must truly want to be an attractive and outgoing person when at the receiving end of such immense bad luck. It is much easier to conceive of yourself as a victim and start blaming everybody and everything for your troubles. It is also interesting to note that later, after the crime, the investigators were unable to find any of Herschel's neighbours who described the boy in less than approving terms.

On the bureaucratic side of things, though, the juggernaut of Kafkaesque logic was inexorably bearing down on Herschel. The plain fact remained that he was an illegal immigrant. It was no good claiming refugee status. As we have seen, the sympathies of foreign governments towards the Jews in Germany were hardly backed up with practical provisions for help and accommodation. Uncle Abraham applied immediately on Herschel's arrival to the Central Committee for Aid to Immigrant Jews to bolster his nephew's request for French residence. It is not clear what, if any, sway this organisation held with the French authorities, and it did not get around to transmitting Abraham's request until the end of January 1937.[15] That was a crucial delay of some four months, but it might be explained by the volume of similar requests the Committee was receiving. We shall never know. When Abraham's request was finally transmitted, the result was that the higher bureaucrats became aware of the illegality of Herschel's entry to France. Up till then Herschel had in his possession a receipt of the application for an identity card. It functioned as an ersatz residence permit, but not after July 1938, when the authorities took the decision to throw Herschel out. This decision was communicated to the police in mid-August, and from that date, Herschel was on the run.

But the growing catastrophe does not end there. When he left Germany, his exit visa which allowed him to return to Hanover, was valid only until 1 June, 1937.[16] In the meantime Herschel's Polish passport had also expired, and without it he could no longer live in Germany anyway, so a further extension of the exit visa was simply impossible.[17] Think what this meant. Having fled Belgium for France, the French decided to eject him. He could not return home to Germany because the Germans would never overlook the fact that he was an alien there, too. The Polish, in the meantime, wise to the fact that the Nazis were attempting to send 'home' all their ethnic Polish Jews, had decreed that all Polish passports should be immediately renewed at the Polish consulate in Germany. This applied to all Poles (i.e. Jews) who had lived outside the country for more than five years.[18] In other words it was precisely aimed at folk like Herschel and his family. To revalidate his Polish passport, Herschel had first to return to Germany (as a German Pole he could not go to the Polish consulate in Paris), but Germany would not let him in. The net was closing.

Herschel tried hard. In May 1937 he *did* go to the Polish consulate, and lied his way into a new passport valid until 7 January 1938. He accomplished this by claiming he had lost his passport and needed a replacement. This meant the Polish government was ignorant of the fact that the vital German exit visa had expired. If they had known, Herschel would not have gotten a passport at all. This reveals considerable ingenuity and not a little *chutzpah* on Herschel's part. This was the first embassy he lied his way into, and there would be another. [19]

Once he had a new Polish passport in his grasp, Herschel straightaway wrote direct to the German ambassador.[20] He lied that his original exit visa was not for emigration to Palestine via Brussels, but for studies in Paris. He said these had lasted longer than expected, and he had now lost his passport into the bargain, so please could he have a new exit (entry) visa. The story had so many holes in it that it would not stand up to even a cursory check, but Herschel was desperately trying to play the best hand he could. That same month of September 1937, Abraham visited the German consulate in Paris, and actually met with a sympathetic response. Yes, since Herschel was not allowed to remain in France, and since he was young and in poor health, it would be best if he returned to his parents in Hanover. It is an illustration of how seriously perturbed both the French and German Grynszpans were by now, that this was cause for celebration. Less than a year earlier, return to Nazi Germany was to be avoided by Herschel at all costs.

The mills of bureaucracy grind slowly, but they grind exceedingly small, and when the inevitable check was made back in Hanover, and communicated to the Germans in Paris, all came to light, and Herschel was told that Germany was now out of bounds to him. Sendel pleaded with the consulate in Paris from Hanover, but to no avail. The Germans were rubbing their hands with delight at having rid themselves of a Jew.

By the beginning of 1938, then, Herschel's ultimate predicament was clear to him. The only place he could possibly go was Poland. According to the Nazis he was a Pole and that was where he belonged. But Herschel had never visited Poland, hardly spoke the language, and knew nobody there. His father's mother, Gitta, lived in Radomsk, but it is not clear if he had ever met her. His maternal grandmother also lived in Poland, but Herschel did not know her, either. There was an aunt who had remarried, but Herschel's experience with uncle Wolf in Brussels doubtless made him balk at the idea of another frosty reception in yet another foreign country. The strain was taking its toll on the boy, and at around this time – the beginning of 1938 – he started talking of suicide.

Cuenot makes much of the fact that the pre-trial experts gave no credence to Herschel's suicidal tendencies, but theirs is cruel and cold objectivity that does not even begin to draw close and take account of Herschel's terrible dilemma. Of course he talked of killing himself, as one might say, 'Oh God, I feel like killing myself.' One never means it until one does it, and even the person who threatens himself and others is mostly ignorant of whether he truly intends it. That instant of truth comes at the end or not at all. Herschel was not an attention-seeker like most *faux* suicides, and he could not impress any authority by promising to do away with himself. That would have suited them just fine, anyway. I think he was sincere and that suicide was certainly an option: that Herschel might have killed himself, but would have rather done everything else first. There comes a time when suicide is simply the most practical option, and when it arrives people tend to kill themselves efficiently and unemotionally, without display. But consider how close Herschel was to his family, how well he loved them and was loved. If anything makes one withdraw from the precipice of self-destruction it is the knowledge of how badly one's death would affect others. Herschel's mad plan to enlist in the French Foreign Legion was abandoned for this very reason: 'I hesitated ... because my parents ... had already lost five children.'[21]

By this stage Herschel was refusing to eat, and the psychological strain was showing on him. Things grew rapidly worse on 11 August, when the expulsion order was communicated to the police, and they started looking for him. Abraham and Chawa were now in a terrible position, as they were harbouring an illegal alien, a wanted man. They were accessories to a crime and liable to prosecution. Cuenot says Herschel lied to uncle Abraham that he had persuaded the French Ministry of the Interior to grant him a residence permit.[22] I do not believe this. There is nothing in Herschel's travails that Abraham had not known about all along. And there is nothing in his nephew's character to suggest such base ingratitude would ever have been considered by him. If Abraham was ignorant of Herschel's situation, why had he gone to the German consulate to plead with them for Herschel to be given a new exit visa? If he thought Herschel had a French residence permit there would have been no need.

What is more, Abraham hardly reacted with anger when Herschel became a fugitive. Instead he responded in a way that had characterised his love and generosity all along. He and Chawa moved again, for Herschel's sake as much as their own, to 6 rue des Petites Ecuries, just around the corner. Herschel remained at the previous address, secreted in a garret room up on the sixth floor of the tenement block, and when the gendarmes raided 8 rue Martel, Herschel was indeed hiding upstairs. All the neighbours knew he was there; none gave him away. The police then descended on Abraham and Chawa at their new place but found nothing.

After that, the heat was off, but Herschel had entered a strange, paranoid world. He was of necessity cooped up alone in the dark attic room during daylight hours, creeping around the streets at night like a feral animal, or stealing over to his aunt and uncle's place at dusk for meals. But even under these conditions he somehow just managed to withstand the strain. For example, Herschel still saw his friends, mainly a young Jewish neighbour called Nathan Kaufman. This implies his nerves were not entirely frayed, and he even ventured out to the sportsclub *L'Aurore* to attend dances, as he had done in the past. All the facts attest to his resilience and fundamental sanity, his refusal to cave in to the monolithic forces of faceless bureaucracy that were closing in on him. This grim period was not the making of an assassin. There would be yet another final straw.

CHAPTER FOUR

THE FINAL STRAW

S omething at last gave way in Herschel on the afternoon of Sunday 6 November. Furthermore, it was directed outwards rather than in on himself, and towards the very people who were helping and caring for him.

Sunday lunch *chez* Abraham and Chawa was usually a pleasant and intimate affair. That this particular occasion was destined to be different is implied by the presence of Mina Berenbaum, wife of Chawa's brother, Beimis, and of the Wykhodzes, Jacques and Basila – Chawa's sister. This was heavy artillery, and it is likely that Chawa had appealed to them to come along to exert some family pressure on Herschel; regarding what, precisely, is a matter of dispute. There are two possibilities, and they are probably linked. Herschel's friend Nathan arrived a little later as well, too late to receive any exact idea of what the quarrel was about, but early enough to be caught in the middle of the uproar. Again, the massed ranks of relatives almost certainly meant the confrontation had been brewing for a while, and we know that it was to do with Herschel's family in Hanover – or right now in no-man's land between Poland and Germany, to where they had been deported by the Nazis.

Herschel, avidly devouring newsprint, was super-aware of the worsening situation of the Jews in Germany. They were caught in the diplomatic crossfire between Berlin and Warsaw. The former wished to repatriate the 50,000 or so Polish Jews resident in Germany and Austria; the latter, almost as anti-semitic, wanted none of them. In March of 1938 the Polish government stole a march on the Nazis by announcing, as we mentioned above, that Poles (i.e. Jews) living abroad were more or less disenfranchised of their old nationality. It was August of that year[1] before the Nazi mentality got its milk teeth into the consequences of the Polish decree. When at last it did, the order depriving 'foreigners' (i.e. Jews) of their residence permits was issued through the police and they began to await the worst. The Grynszpans, no fools, had seen what was ahead, and Ryfka had already made a couple of trips to Poland that year, visiting relatives and metaphorically packing the family parachute.

Nonetheless, when the deportation came it was unexpected, shocking, violent and inhuman. Herschel must have begun to boil over in Paris on the Wednesday, which was 2 November. In the post that morning he had received a postcard from his sister that she had managed to send from Zbaszyn in Poland, and which relayed the horrible news of the family's removal from Germany. Herschel had ample time to brood over this new information while pacing his garret room, and must have announced something to his aunt and uncle in advance of the explosive Sunday lunch. The postcard was discovered on Herschel after his arrest, and it graphically described the events of the evening of Thursday 28 October. Another postcard, more desperate and pleading, and written on the day Herschel shot vom Rath, was intercepted by the police when it arrived in Paris. Clearly, Herschel had been successful in contacting his family at *poste restante*, somewhere in Poland:

Dear [Herschel],

We received your dear letter. Up until now nothing has changed our very unhappy situation. I'll continue with the description... On Saturday morning we were ordered to get out [of the freight wagons] somewhere in the deserted countryside. It was a nerve-wracking spectacle – the manner in which we were chased through fields and forests. After that we were forced to settle in barracks. Those who have money can lodge in private places. A committee from Warsaw has come here. These people do what they can for us. But believe me, [Herschel], we won't be able to stand this much longer. Since we left we have not yet been able to undress... Everything depends on the Jewish community. We haven't yet received money from you. What do they say there about what will happen to us? We can't go any further.

Berta.[2]

There was a post-script from Herschel's father addressed to Abraham and Chawa:

Dear Brother and Sister-in-Law,

We are in a very sad situation. We are poor and in misery. We don't get enough to eat. You, too, once were in need. I beg you, dear brother, to think of us. We don't have the strength to endure this. You mustn't forget us in this situation.

Sindel.[3]

Though Herschel never received this postcard, it is revealing of the matters in question at Sunday lunch. Firstly, it is obvious that Herschel had promised to send money – easier said than done, and likely the impulsive promise of an overwrought teenager. It is likely, too, that uncle Abraham was attempting to point out the sheer impracticality of wiring money to one family out of 12,000 people in a field somewhere in Poland. I believe Abraham was guilty of being reasonable when that was the last thing Herschel was interested in. From somewhere Cuenot seems to have picked up the idea that Abraham was surly and mean ('niggardliness', he calls it[4]) but from where is difficult to imagine. From well before Herschel crossed the Belgian border, Abraham had bent over backwards to do all he could for the boy. There is every sign that fatherhood, even of this late and tangential sort, was a joy to him and his wife. He must have been on very good terms with his brother in the first place to have accepted responsibility for his nephew. There was another Grynszpan brother, Salomon, who lived in Paris but whom Abraham was not fond of and hardly ever saw, which suggests that he did nothing simply out of family obligation.

Secondly, the fact that Abraham insisted on giving Herschel 200 francs when the boy finally stormed out of the flat further points up Abraham's generosity and strength of feeling. He was holding what he felt to be a very important line: the Red Cross and the Jewish organisations were doing all they could, and it was best to await further developments before pitching money into the void. It is difficult to disentangle all the details of the departure from Abraham's flat, but the whole drama was really about Herschel wanting to get a handle on his uncontrollable emotions, and venting his anger and frustration on those closest to him – the only people who could begin to understand what he was going through.

When Herschel stormed out, the family implored Nathan to stay with him, and the youth duly ran off down the street in pursuit of his tormented friend. Nathan trotted alongside Herschel, attempting to calm him down, trying to reason with him. He met with some measure of success, and Herschel agreed to accompany him to a tea dance at *L'Aurore*, near the cirque d'Hiver. For all Herschel's histrionics and his wish to be left alone with his pain, he was glad of Nathan's company, and the boys remained at the sportsclub all afternoon, although Herschel was in no mood for jollity.[5] His presence there does suggest that he was fundamentally a sociable fellow, and not someone who preferred to hide away, the better to nurse a grievance. Herschel's actions seem definitely to have been a reaction to the pressure he was under rather than any conscious or deliberate planning either of a scene or anything else that followed.

By the evening, Herschel could be talked to again: looking at pretty girls had probably taken the edge off his mood. But there was nothing Nathan could do to persuade him to return to his uncle's flat. In fact Herschel was adamant, in a strange and interesting way, saying something to Nathan that opens onto the second area of possible disagreement at the ill-fated luncheon. 'I will not go back,' he said. 'I'd rather die like a dog from hunger, than go back on my decision.'[6]

Later, after vom Rath's assassination, the Nazis tried to make much of the Sunday conflagration, and this quote from Nathan was key to their argument that, although the quarrel may have been about money, that was a secondary subject. The true flashpoint between Herschel and his anxious relatives was supposedly his announcement that he had decided to to assassinate a German. 'I'd rather die like a dog from hunger' sounds as if he is refusing further hospitality from his aunt and uncle, to be sure, but what of his 'decision' which sounds far more ominous? Perhaps the Nazis had a point.

Perhaps not: this was the time during which suicide was a regular feature of Herschel's conversation with his nearest and dearest in Paris, and it is possible he was practising a little moral extortion on Abraham, by threatening to do away with himself if his uncle did not wire the money to Sendel. Actually, it is not clear there even *was* any money. Herschel's father had supposedly sent Abraham 3,000 francs for his son's upkeep when the youngster first arrived in Paris. But just how that amount could have been smuggled out of Germany is difficult to imagine (not only was such a sum arguably beyond Sendel's meagre resources, but the Germans would have noticed, since all assets owned by Jews had had to be registered in order that they could be stolen by the Nazis a little later). Cuenot reports that Herschel himself had 500 francs somewhere for a new coat.[7] If he was so determined to help out his family, he could have sent that money. In other words, perhaps cash was not the crux of the matter.

Yet if Herschel's decision was to jump off a bridge, then what was he doing hanging around at a dance, cooling off? There must surely be an element of reasonableness in the supposition that he had threatened some spectacular action aimed at focusing attention on the deportations of Jews from Germany, although it is certain even Herschel himself at this point had no idea exactly what it might be.[8] Nonetheless, even the hint of it would have been enough to scare his relatives witless: if Herschel came into any kind of contact with the authorities, it was not just curtains for him but deep trouble for Abraham and Chawa, who would be had up for harbouring a fugitive. Plainly, Herschel was so unhinged at this point that his customary consideration for those around him was impaired. He was an impulsive boy at the best of times, and this was part of his charm; but it could tip him briefly into rage and paranoia if he was, as now, hopelessly cornered.

Herschel and Nathan parted around 7 o'clock that evening, after he had again (and angrily) refused to go back to his aunt and uncle's flat.[9] The fact that it was not a true breakdown in relations from Abraham and Chawa's point of view is illustrated by the search parties that were sent out to scout all Herschel's local haunts that evening. They looked high and low: in his garret, at the café *Tout Va Bien* and at *L'Aurore*. Nathan too joined in the hunt, but Herschel was nowhere to be found.

He was in fact on his way to check into an hotel, the *Ideal-Suez*, and once more there is an innocent explanation for this as well as a more sinister one. And then there is the real reason. The innocent explanation is that the last thing Herschel wanted was the solicitous attentions of his family, so he was laying out a little money for privacy. On the other hand he could have just gone back to his garret. At least then, knowing where he was, his relatives would be partly re-assured when he told them to go away.

They were out of their minds with worry that he would do something stupid, and to himself rather than somebody else.

So why then an hotel? Was he up to something? Is there a sinister explanation? Was he trying to disassociate Abraham and Chawa from what he was going to do? Again, one would have to argue not. If Herschel committed a serious crime, his relatives would be involved no matter what. An assassination could be plotted just as well from the comfort of one's own room as (rather more expensively) from a nice hotel on the Boulevard Strasbourg. Also, it was not as though he was planning champagne and dancing girls for his last night of liberty. On the contrary, this was to be Herschel's hellish and hallucinatory dark night of the soul.

In truth, he didn't know where he was going, or what he was doing. Emotionally, he wanted to make himself small and hide away from everyone and everything. At the same time, though, his unconscious soul was driving him relentlessly forward on its own obscure journey towards action. Something was building in him, and circumstances that evening were conspiring to trip the trigger of his angst, and transform him from a limbo-like existence in neurotic space to an active one in existential space. Herschel's past and future, his character and experiences, his frustrations and worries and rage, were all converging on a single point, and he went to the hotel because he felt this. He did not go there with a plan: the plan was rushing out into the matrix of his soul, and needed the breathing space of an unfamiliar bed in a strange room to do its work. Herschel was on automatic pilot, keeping an appointment with a part of himself that was about to be born.

As Herschel wandered the darkened streets, aimlessly but also with purpose, tightly packed within himself, turning over and over in his head the voices and events of the recent past, his peripheral vision latched onto a shopsign. Perhaps it was the name, *A La Fine Lame* ('The Sharp Blade'), that caught his attention and made some deep, moodily apt impression on him. He lingered in front of the store and looked mindlessly at the dull blue glint of the revolvers and pistols in the window, perfect little objects with all the sexiness and power of transformation stored in their delicate lines and compact heft. Certainly the hypnotic sight of so much raw potential galvanised Herschel's unconscious in some way, for he continued east along the rue de Faubourg St Martin only until the next left turn. The hotel *Ideal-Suez* was right there, across the street a little further down on Boulevard Strasbourg, and he promptly checked in, paying cash in advance and claiming to be Heinrich Halter – an Aryan alter-ego? – eighteen years old and from Hanover. He apologised for having no identification papers, and then went out. Nobody knows where, although the concierge assumed it was to collect his luggage from the Gare de l'Est, where the train from Germany had not long before arrived.[10]

Once again we see Herschel lying with utter efficiency and without breaking into a sweat. His coolness, allied with his youth and good looks, dispelled any misgivings on the part of the hotel-owner's daughter who received him. But this must not make us assume that all was cold and calculated on Herschel's part. He had a facility for invention; he was a natural actor; when he felt he had to do something he slipped without hesitation into character and gave a bravura performance. It was this talent that would firstly give rise to a certain pomposity of behaviour when he became famous overnight, and secondly would just about stop the teenager from cracking under interrogation, in France and then later in Germany. It was this very talent that allowed him the leeway to save his life and grow into the very serious character he later became, when he single-handedly scuppered the Nazis' plans for him from within the Third Reich.

It was during that restless night that Herschel's troubled, grieving soul balanced all, and finally brought all to mind. It was more than dreams he had as he tossed and turned, oblivious to the light he had left on in his room. What he experienced were visions, more real than the wakeful dream of life. The weeping faces of his family loomed toward him pleading that he save them, and stormtroopers grabbed him by the throat, shaking his life from him. Crowds of

Germans surrounded Herschel, screaming over and over that he was a dirty Jew. He saw Germans who emerged from his father's shop kicked and spat at by their countrymen: 'You are damned! You are selling the German people to the Jews!' hollered the crowd. There was the crackle of machine gun fire in a dark field and people running, and his sister crying out to him. And again and again, like a scratched record, Herschel watched himself linger outside the gunshop, then push open the door and enter.

He awoke three times, deafened by the noise of his pounding heart which he vainly attempted to calm by massaging his chest. Sometime towards dawn sleep finally claimed him, and swooningly in his dreams the same question flickered across his mind's eye: 'What have we done to deserve such a fate?' And to it always he supplied the plaintive answer: 'I do not know'.

The morning found him exhausted. His hands shook as Herschel lifted to his lips the cup of strong black coffee he had ordered from room service. But something in him had changed. Despite his physical weariness and his tattered nerves, Herschel was oddly calm. His mind no longer raced as it had done during the night. It was as if the storm had blown itself out, having flattened all the obstacles between Herschel and his destination. The anger at his relatives had dissipated, and however wild he had been before, Herschel's decision allowed him to sail into the calm seas of forgiveness. Before he left the hotel, early, just after dawn, he wrote a postcard to uncle Abraham. It was one that had on it Herschel's portrait, probably taken at a fair or by a street photographer. It somehow made the message doubly personal, and definitively final. 'With God's help' he began, in Hebrew:

> My dear relatives, I couldn't do otherwise. God must forgive me. My heart bleeds when I think of our tragedy and that of the 12,000 Jews. I have to protest in a way that the whole world hears my protest, and this I intend to do.
> I beg your forgiveness. Herschel.[11]

And with that, he stepped out into the brightening November day, an almost-man leaving the frightened boy behind.

CHAPTER FIVE

THE NEWS TODAY

Ernst vom Rath almost always arrived early at his office on the first
floor of the German embassy at 78 rue de Lille. Today, 7
November, he made sure he was the first attaché in the building, for he had some important work to complete; work it was essential
that nobody else in the embassy was privy to. Recapitulated below is the
rumour, concerning the nature of that work, that Cuenot rehearsed
in his thesis. I think it is very much more than a rumour; Cuenot did
not, although it is difficult to see why on the evidence he cites.

In 1939, Alain Cuenot was a doctor attached to the 315th Army Corps
in the Vosges Mountains – holding the line south of the 'impassable'
Ardennes forest, where a few months later the German armour would
make its almost unopposed dash into the heart of France. It was here
that the incident described in the prologue took place. Mme
Collignon, wife of a captured Nazi spy, was brought to Cuenot having
attempted suicide by drug overdose. The story told to Dr Cuenot by
the young intelligence officers who came to interrogate her as she
recovered is a remarkable one.

Mme Collignon's husband was merely one of many spies the Nazis had activated behind French lines, for Hitler was planning his invasion of France and the Low Countries from early on. It was not his main priority, but he felt it essential to secure his western flank before he turned east toward his true enemy, Russia. Hitler was also understandably perturbed by the strength of the defences along the Maginot line. This amazing construction of caseworks, interspaced with fortresses every five miles along its considerable length, was invulnerable. Garrisons within could survive unsupplied for months, and were richly equipped with devastating armaments.[1]

After annexing the Sudetenland, Hitler knew just how costly an assault on such defences would be. It was not that an attack had been mounted in Czechoslovakia, but a test bombardment on the captured defences in that country had shown their indestructibility, and the potential cost in German lives in attempting to breach them.[2] For this reason, it was imperative that Hitler be able to follow intimately the movements of the Allied forces within France so his main force could sneak in relatively unopposed. For this plan to succeed, Hitler needed intelligence of Allied concentrations and directions of movement: up-to-date, detailed and extensive. Secret transmitter sites were thus established throughout France.

The French knew this, but could do little about it. Intercepting Collignon was something of a coup, but he had only been apprehended by chance. What they needed, said the intelligence officers with whom Cuenot spoke, was a list of all the transmitters and all the operators. They would not obtain that from Collignon, since elementary spooking decreed that each spy knew only one other, or even none at all.

That vital list had almost fallen into their possession a year earlier, on 7 November 1938, from an anti-Nazi German spy situated within the German embassy in Paris. The agent, working closely with French intelligence – the *Deuxième Bureau* – was the man the Nazis had made responsible for ensuring the radios were delivered to various railway stations throughout France. There, the transmitters were deposited in left-luggage offices, from where the French Nazi operatives would collect them. The agent would return to Paris with the baggage receipt as proof of delivery. The two would never actually have to meet, and this suited the agent very well.

Thus the anti-Nazi agent in the German embassy was in a perfect position seriously to hamper, if not to destroy, Nazi plans for the invasion of France. This is no exaggeration: the defences in terms of troops, artillery and aircraft inside France were considerable. To take them on would have meant a long and bloody campaign for Hitler, with final success unassured. It was only by means of an elaborate feint, drawing off the Allies' best troops towards Belgium and then sweeping into France through the Ardennes, that Hitler could hope to achieve the superfast victory – the *blitzkrieg* – that he did.

The German double agent had been able to contact and recruit himself into the service of the *Deuxième Bureau* through the offices of the francophile anti-Nazi German whose name we have already come across: Maître von Bose. By now the daring young man was reporting directly to the head of French military intelligence, Colonel Gauche, and on this sunny November day was preparing his final, conclusive act against the Nazi dictatorship he had learned to despise. On that very afternoon he was to hand over the list containing the names of Nazi agents and the sites of their transmitters to the French. It was almost the most critical piece of information existent in Europe at this tense and delicate time nearly a year before outbreak of the Second World War. The courageous agent's name was Baron Ernst vom Rath.

That is the tale related by Cuenot, and he dismisses it more or less out of hand. Which is odd, because the more closely one examines the possibility that vom Rath was indeed an anti-Nazi agent, the more persuasive and probable it becomes. For his part, Cuenot seems to have decided vom Rath was not (though he is happy to state vom Rath was certainly no Nazi), but only on the basis of several rather slight reasons: the fact that the Baron was 'frank and open' in character, from an upper class family, well-off, not in a position to be blackmailed, and patriotic.

This is unconvincing. For example, 'frank and open' does not exclude shrewd and intelligent, qualities vom Rath certainly possessed. If he was spying for the French, he would be smart enough to ensure he appeared a normal fellow to his workmates, and would to the best of his ability try to be popular with them. The idea that spies should act shiftily and speak from the corners of their mouths is not only an unrealistic cliché, but counterproductive in practice. Frank and open, then, is just what vom Rath would have needed to *seem* to be.

Cuenot only seems to conceive of vom Rath becoming involved in espionage against his will. Thus, he could be induced to 'treachery' only because he needed money (and the French could pay him well), or because the *Deuxième Bureau* had some incriminating information with which to blackmail him. Cuenot is so intent on refuting the allegations of homosexuality Herschel later made against vom Rath that it clouds his judgment in this instance. The French may not have needed to blackmail vom Rath at all. My contention is that they had no idea of approaching him; that rather vom Rath approached the French, using his good friend Maître von Bose as an initial go-between. Von Bose was trusted by French intelligence, and they would trust someone referred to them by him.

Cuenot's contention that as vom Rath was 'patriotic' he would not stoop to treachery surely begs the question. What did it mean to be a patriotic German when your country was commanded by a criminal government with a megalomaniac at its helm? Many other young, professional and 'well brought-up' German anti-Nazis were already actively attempting to overthrow Hitler, as anybody who has read Christabel Bielenberg's book will know. For them, patriotism lay in restoring Germany to herself and rescuing her from the course on which the Nazis had set the country. In other words, treason was a matter of perspective, and to vom Rath the real treachery would have been to collude with and serve the Nazi régime. It is also impossible, given his social position, career and sensibility, that vom Rath had not early on already come into contact with the anti-Nazis who had been risking their lives in pursuit of democracy in Germany since shortly after Hitler snatched power. So far as vom Rath's character is concerned, then, there is nothing really to argue against his clandestine anti-Nazi activities, and everything to argue in favour of them.

Turning to practicalities and historical evidence, one again finds Cuenot's denials to be built on unsound foundations. For example, he says that a search of the *Deuxième Bureau*'s files in the Vincennes Chateaux after the war turned up nothing that implicated vom Rath in any such espionage. But to begin with it was not Cuenot who made the search: General de Crosse-Brissac, who was in charge of the French Army Historical Service, ordered one of his officers to make it.[3] This officer would naturally have reported back to General Crosse-Brissac before handing anything over to a provincial doctor, and any finds would then have been closely vetted by the *Deuxième Bureau* itself.

We must also consider that after the war there were many spying activities still in operation: Nazis remained at large and were being carefully lured into the open; half of Germany was in Soviet hands, and many of the other names in any files containing references to vom Rath might still have been working in the field. To release the files could have jeopardised the security of who knows how many agents, and countless 'live' activities. Furthermore, intelligence services do not customarily release information to anybody who asks unless they have to. Perhaps now, after the end of the Cold War, is the time for a proper search to be conducted, although by now it may be too late. Finally, even as Cuenot himself admits, 'It is not customary ... for the *Deuxième Bureau* to leave traces in dealings of that sort'.[4] In other words, he admits that the fruitless search on which his conclusion rests proved absolutely nothing: the French would never have compromised vom Rath by having his name noted anywhere in the first place. He would have been a tremendously valuable asset to them, much too important to risk by holding papers on him. With possibly a war and invasion ahead, moreover, it was doubtless in the interests of the French to destroy any files – if they existed in the first place – that might have fallen into German hands.

Next, Cuenot says that he does not believe vom Rath ever undertook any of the journeys he supposedly made to deliver transmitters around France. The reason he gives is that when he asked vom Rath's family about his trips, they claimed no knowledge of them – as if the vom Raths would ever have been informed, as civilians, of activities of that kind. It is unlikely that anybody else at the embassy even knew where vom Rath was going, if and when he went, never mind his parents back in Germany. The trips would have lasted less than a day, anyway; hardly worth writing home about, even if it was permitted. Fisher and Read.[5] They even manage to find a refutation for Herschel's allegations of homosexuality against vom Rath in the fact that on the date when the Baron was supposed to be sequestered in an hotel room with Herschel, he was in fact out of Paris. Delivering a transmitter, perhaps. It was a weekday, so why was he not at work? This would please Cuenot on one level and dismay him on another. In addition, it is not clear that vom Rath would have been required to deliver all of the radios. That was more of a field agent's job. To the Nazis, vom Rath was a manager, an operator, too valuable and highly qualified to spend much of his time lugging heavy equipment all over France. From his own point of view, if vom Rath only delivered a few of the transmitters it would have been more secure for him. If there was not a perfect fit between his supply and their arrest, then when the Nazi agents he betrayed were apprehended, it would be more difficult for German intelligence to trace all the captures back to vom Rath. He had his own safety to consider, and there is nothing in his character to suggest recklessness. Had there been, the French would not have gone near him.

Lastly, and again somewhat unbelievably, Cuenot claims that the examining magistrate in Herschel's trial – Judge Tesnière – never mentioned vom Rath in the context of being a Nazi agent. This has to count as sheer naïvety. For a start, the Germans were attempting to organise a massive propaganda exercise, a show trial of a 'dirty Jew' who had ruthlessly assassinated in cold blood a fine Nazi and German patriot. The whole enterprise would have been shot to ribbons if it emerged that vom Rath was working on behalf of French intelligence. That is *not* to say, though, that the Nazis were ignorant of vom Rath's activities. I believe they discovered what he was up to even before he died, and that it may have cost him his life, as I will argue below. But they would never have disclosed the fact, least of all to the French. And even if Judge Tesnière was aware of vom Rath's true identity, there is nothing to suggest he would have risked angering the Nazis by saying it aloud.

Cuenot sketches an impartial picture of Tesnière who, it must be said, was in an extremely delicate position in this case. He had to uphold justice and at the same time appease the Nazis, who were glowering at France and armed to the teeth into the bargain. Schwab, though, is much less charitable to Tesnière, representing him as a shit-eating Nazi collaborator who helped the Germans above and beyond the call of duty or necessity. In either case there was no way Tesnière would risk ruining a trial that could have made the Nazis look with kindness on France, just for the sake of a Jewish delinquent.

There is other evidence, which we shall examine later, that argues for vom Rath's involvement with French intelligence and makes perfect sense of many details of the story that otherwise do not quite fit together. Perhaps vom Rath allowed his secretary to show in the young man who arrived with 'important papers' on the morning of 8 November because he was expecting just such a visit. Did he think the final baggage receipt had arrived? Or did he assume the appointment with French intelligence had been moved forward, or that the visitor was to instruct him on arrangements for the 'drop'? Whatever he assumed, it cost him his life.

As vom Rath was sitting down at his desk, across town Herschel was emerging, blinking, into the sunny November day. He pulled straight his smart raincoat, turned the collar gangster-wise, and set off briskly up the street toward the gun shop. He got there at 8.35 a.m., just as the owner's wife, Mme Carpe, was opening up.[6] She called her husband, surprised at receiving a customer so early, and M Carpe came through from the rear of the shop. He looked askance at Herschel, wondering why a mere boy would be wanting to buy a firearm. But once again, Herschel was instinctively word perfect. He simply took out his wallet, full of uncle Abraham's 200 francs, and the 500 he already had for a new coat, and presenting M Carpe with sight of a convincing bankroll, stated that he had to carry large amounts of money to the bank for his father, that this was known, and that he was afraid of being robbed in the street.

This was good enough for M Carpe, and indeed good enough for French law, which was stupifyingly lax on gun control. If one had the money and was of 'sound mind', howitzers and machine guns could readily be had, and it is little wonder that France suffered from astonishingly high rates of armed crime. The two simple requirements to legalise the transaction were for the seller to fill in an official registration to keep, and for the buyer to complete a form and take it to the nearest police station.[7]

Herschel knew nothing about guns, but Carpe explained. Since he assumed Herschel wanted protection from possibly more than one attacker, he looked for a piece that would answer the demand perfectly. He selected a weapon that could be stowed unobtrusively about the person, but from which a single round would be enough to disable. He handed Herschel a five-chambered 6x35mm hammerless revolver. That is like a .25 semi-automatic, which with a long cartridge is extremely powerful, more like a snub-nosed .38. It was, in other words, a very deadly weapon.[8]

Herschel paid 210 francs for it, and handed over another 35 francs for a box of cartridges. M Carpe showed Herschel the action and how to load the gun, then double-wrapped the empty weapon

in brown paper and secured the package with elastic bands. The last
thing the owner said was to be sure to go immediately to the police
station and register the weapon. Herschel replied that was exactly
where he was headed, and he duly set off up Boulevard Strasbourg
again, toward the northern end of which was located precinct headquarters.

But once out of sight of M Carpe, Herschel changed direction.
He went to a place he knew, the café *Tout Va Bien*, and disappeared
into the washroom. He locked himself inside a cubicle, unwrapped
the gun, and loaded it. Then Herschel flushed the toilet and walked
back through the café, bidding good day to the waiter setting tables.
On the street again, Herschel turned towards the Métro (Strasbourg-
St Denis) and bought a ticket to take him to Solferino (line 8;
change at Madeleine for line 12), nearest station to the German
embassy.[9] It is interesting to note that Herschel tried to buy a return
ticket, but could not because it had just turned 9.00 a.m. Where or
what he thought he was going to return to is anybody's guess.

From the station he walked up rue de Lille to the embassy. It was
a large building with several anonymous entrances, so Herschel
asked the gendarme on duty outside which he should go through
to apply for an entry visa to Germany. The gendarme, Autret, correctly informed him that he needed the consulate, not the embassy,
as Herschel was well aware. This is the only detail that testifies to
Herschel's nervousness. It almost certainly shocked him out of it,
though, since the policeman could now well have prevented his
entry if he felt like it. Herschel had to act fast now after making such
a blunder, and quickly strode up to a man of dignified appearance
who had come through one of the embassy portals. He asked the
gentleman where he could find the ambassador, and was waved
wordlessly toward the door. It was an action that saved the life of this
man, for he was Count Welczeck, the ambassador himself, and
Herschel's target of preference. He descended the steps to take his
customary morning stroll, and Herschel disappeared inside to alter
the course of history.

Once Herschel had been shown up to the first floor by the wife of the concierge, he bluffed his way into vom Rath's office with surprising ease. It is true that vom Rath was the only attaché present so early in the morning, but it was by no means a sure thing that Herschel would have been permitted to see him. The secretary, Nagorka, could have told the youth to return later, or instructed him to wait. That he did not is due to Herschel's claim that he was carrying important documents, and that he had to hand them over personally.

It was a tragic coincidence that Herschel's words clicked with Nagorka and propelled him in the direction of vom Rath's office. The reason was this: of all the countries that maintained embassies in Paris, only the USSR and Germany took advantage of the rules of extra-territoriality to maintain an espionage desk.[10] The fact that Herschel, once he presented himself as a spy or an informer, was shown directly to vom Rath is likely to mean only one thing: vom Rath must have been the officer who ran the local informants. He had a pedigree after all, since his uncle, Roland Koester, had ran the intelligence desk during his own time as ambassador in Paris. Herschel, in his guise as a spy, would certainly not have been shown in to just any official. It was pure dumb luck for him that vom Rath was in the building. We already know what vom Rath was probably doing there that early.

All there is to follow in this sad and ironic incident is the banality of the attack itself. After Nagorka had left Herschel and vom Rath alone, the German apparently said something like, 'I believe you have a document for me?' There might have been a password, there might not. At any rate Herschel replied, 'You're a filthy German, and in the name of 12,000 persecuted Jews, here is the document!' With that he pulled out his revolver and took aim at vom Rath, who sprang from his chair. Never having fired a gun before, and this one having quite a kick, Herschel's arm naturally jerked up with each round. The bullets sprayed wildly around the room, but at point-blank range it was inevitable that vom Rath would be hit. And so he was, twice, once in the stomach and once in the chest, up near his left shoulder. The momentum of his leap toward Herschel carried vom Rath forward, and he managed to land a good punch on Herschel's cheek. Herschel, stunned by what he had done, and quite at a loss what next to do, threw the weapon at vom Rath (it missed) as the latter walked to the door, using the few seconds' grace before the impact of the bullets took hold to call for help. Nagorka and Kreuger were pounding along the corridor, and when vom Rath saw them he announced simply and calmly that he was wounded.

More embassy employees quickly rushed into his office, attempting to help and comfort vom Rath, who was quietly bleeding to death on the rug. Others laid hands on Herschel, who put up no fight at all, and someone picked the gun up from the floor. The price tag was still tied around the trigger-guard. Later, Herschel claimed that vom Rath had called him a 'dirty Jew'. 'Was that before or after you shot him?' he was asked. Herschel said he couldn't recall. He mumbled and hesitated. In other words he was lying. Such a phrase would never have passed the lips of a man like vom Rath.

CHAPTER SIX

THE NIGHT OF BROKEN GLASS

A decade and a half earlier, in 1923, during Hitler's street-fighting days, he and his stormtroopers had attempted a coup in Bavaria, spiritual home of National Socialism. The date was 9 November. The group, numbering 3,000, marched from the beer hall where it was gathered toward the War Ministry, but was met on the way by the regular army, wielding rifles. Röhm's SA were already surrounded. Flushed with drink, and variously armed, the SS decided to charge the troops, and sixteen paid for it with their lives. The rout was general, and eye-witnesses reported they had never seen Hitler move so fast (in the opposite direction). The bungled assault became known as the *Bürgerbraükeller*, or beerhall putsch, and that day became enshrined in Nazi memory as a martyr's holiday, to be celebrated annually as *Tag der Bewegung*, 'Nazi Day'.[1] It was especially unlucky for the German and Austrian Jews that Baron Ernst vom Rath, the great Nazi hero, died two days after he was shot, at just after 4 o'clock in the afternoon, 9 November 1938.

The good news was relayed to Hitler as he and his veteran cronies were finishing their commemorative feast in the Old City Hall in Munich. Regardless of how much Hitler knew about the real vom Rath, there was genuine pleasure in his demise: a dead diplomat was in this case much more useful to the Nazis than a living one. Immediately upon his passing, poor vom Rath was promoted – though not by very much and maybe even grudgingly (up about three minor grades to *Legationsrat* or Counsellor of Legation) – to make Herschel's crime appear the more grave and deliberate. Hitler, seated next to Josef Goebbels, PhD, whispered animatedly to him, but the glowing ears of those around managed to pick up only one phrase: that the SA should 'have its fling'.[2] Hitler then got up and left with more than usual flounce and melodramatics, indicating that he was beside himself with rage. Right on cue Goebbels stood up and delivered one of his classic anti-semitic speeches: demented and foaming, but with an undercurrent of pragmatic evil, and some simple hidden commands. He declared that, in spite of the outrage perpetrated on Germany by the vile Jews, the Nazi party was not to demonstrate against Jews within Germany by burning their synagogues or destroying their shops and businesses. Absolutely that was not to take place as the result of Nazi mobilisations. The message was clear enough: don't get caught, not that there was much danger of it, since the police would not dare intervene, and might even condone what was about to be unleashed on an innocent civilian population.

The *Gauleiters* (local party bosses) present at the celebration straightaway rushed to find telephones and alert their offices what must be done. Reinhard Heydrich, chief of the SD (Security Service) was staying at a nearby hotel and did not know what was happening until he saw the glow from a burning synagogue illuminate his room. Thus it was not until nearly midnight that he had an underling, Müller, telex to all SS and SD offices the following guidelines:

Berlin Nr 234404 9.11.2355
To all State Police offices and State Police administrative offices.
– To director or his deputy.
This teletype message is to be transmitted immediately in the most rapid way.
    1. Actions against the Jews and in particular against their synagogues will occur in a short time, in all of Germany. They are not to be hindered. However, it is to be made certain, in agreement with the ordinary police, that plundering and similar lawbreaking will be held to a minimum.
    2. Insofar that important archive material is present in the synagogues, it is to be secured by immediate measures.
    3. The seizure of some 20-30,000 Jews in the Reich is to be prepared. Wealthy Jews above all are to be chosen. More detailed directives will appear in the course of this night.
    4. If, in the course of this action, Jews are found in possession of arms then the sharpest measures are to be employed. Special troops of the SS as well as the general SS can be drawn into the total action. In any case the direction of the actions through the State police is to be assured by proper measures.

Addenda for State Police Cologne:
    In the synagogue of Cologne there is especially important material. This is to be made safe, immediately, by the quickest measures in agreement with the Security Services.[3]

Other directives transmitted that night added various new and detailed orders: the ordinary police were to stand by (or rather stand down) by order of the führer; the press were to be called in; destruction was permitted but looting was not; local mayors and officials were to assist in the targeting of Jewish premises, and said premises to be daubed with slogans such as, 'Revenge for the murder of vom Rath,' 'Death to international Jewry' and 'No understanding with nations under the sway of Jews'.[4] Even if the Nazi goons could not spell these, the message was clear, and proud. The directive not to be caught smashing and fire-raising in uniform arrived too late, and many party units were flying their flags from trashed shops and warehouses, but it hardly mattered.

Nothing can convey the horror of that terrible night. Kristallnacht refers of course to the billions of marks' worth of broken plate glass over which the gentile population had to walk to work the next morning (before the rioting began afresh after the stormtroopers had rested from their nightshift). But the name also refers to an idea of purification, a purging of the German body politic of the Jewish infection. As such it was a harbinger of the holocaust to come, and as the first and most public display of organised state evil, it remains the flagship episode in that chapter of the devil's project. The beatings and humiliations of that night will forever live in calumny.

When Goebbels heard of the first Jewish death at about 2 in the morning, he said, 'Oh dear'. But the figures speak for themselves: 30,000 Jews, almost all of them male, were arrested and sent to Buchenwald, Dachau and Sachsenhausen (later Herschel's home). Most returned home after six weeks, thin and frostbitten, but hundreds had died in the meantime. During Kristallnacht many Jews committed suicide. It is difficult to separate who killed themselves from who were murdered at the height of the frenzy, but at least six Jewish women perished by their own hand, and there are reports of entire families choosing to die together rather than be taken by the Nazis. There were only four rapes, which is surprising, but the anti-miscegenation law was taken seriously by the Nazis. Those who committed the rapes were later tried under this legislation, not under that which declared rape a crime.

7,500 Jewish stores were defenestrated, at least 267 synagogues razed, and almost every Jewish cemetery set about with sledge-hammers. In addition, 177 private homes were gutted. [S 27] But these are just numbers that cannot do justice to the hellishness experienced by those turned out of doors by thugs in the middle of the night. The image of old men on their hands and knees scrubbing the streets with toothbrushes, the while surrounded by jeering crowds, is an appropriate image to keep in mind when attempting to adumbrate the events of 9 and 10 November, 1938. Indeed, this is the central image of Arthur Miller's recent play, *Broken Glass*. It is set in America in the same month, when a New York Jewish house-wife develops a strange paralysis in her legs and grows afraid of her husband who tells her not to worry about Hitler. He cannot under-stand her fascination with a particular photograph she has seen in a newspaper:

> I can't get it out of my mind. On their knees on the side-walk, two old men. And there's fifteen or twenty people on the sidewalk standing in a circle laughing at them scrub-bing with toothbrushes.[6]

Miller's point, of course, is that everyone is affected by this, whether they realise it or not. Except for the heroine of the play, who physically feels the pain, the rest of the world is too spritu-ally dull to sympathise, and this complacency will guarantee the reality of the coming World War.

It was not just the Jewish population that was terrified, though. Kristallnacht was also an object lesson for the German gentiles, few of whom stood by in support of the Nazi gangs on that night and the next day, and most of whom were made sick to their stomachs and scared stiff by the atrocities. Read and Fisher have collected a wealth of anecdotal stories and eye-wit-ness accounts from ordinary Germans, attesting to their fright and disgust. Many who had emerged to see what was going on and had the temerity to be unenthusiastic were arrested by the plainclothed Gestapo agents mingling in every crowd.[7] The tech-nical evidence that the riots were not, as Goebbels claimed the next day, a spontaneous expression of revulsion on behalf of the German people at the foul assassination of vom Rath, is simple and clear.

Firstly why, after vom Rath died, did the population wait six hours, until 3 in the morning, before all over the country concertedly going to work attacking Jewish people and premises? Secondly, why just as suddenly stop and then await the next afternoon before unleashing a similarly co-ordinated second wave of riots. And why, if they were ordinary civilians, did they dress up in Nazi uniforms to perform the destruction? Only the Nazi party had the manpower and the communications to organise so rapidly and on such a scale. The expression on the face of most of the rest of Germany was one of sadness, and behind it a feeling of awful foreboding.

While the population was, perforce, intimidated unto silence, a few elements of the church and the army were not.[8] From the pulpit, Pastor Julius von Jan condemned the Nazi actions, declaring,

> Houses of worship, sacred to others, have been burned down with impunity – men who have loyally served our nation and conscientiously done their duty have been thrown into concentration camps simply because they belong to a different race. Our nation's infamy is bound to bring about divine punishment.[9]

He was beaten and transported to a concentration camp for his pains. It cannot be denied that most churchmen had sworn oaths of allegiance to the führer. Nevertheless there was a felt and tangible, if muted, condemnation from the population at large. It is significant that Julius Streicher, Gauleiter of Franconia and publisher of the anti-Semitic newspaper *Der Stürmer* was led to editorialise that Germans should not show too much compassion for the Jews.[10]

After Kristallnacht a massive leafleting began, reaching Germans in all walks of life, urging them to denounce and rise up against Hitler. This was probably the work of the communists, but it met with more sympathy than usual. Certainly the army did not yet realise what it was up against. It is difficult ever to see an army as a liberal force, especially the German, with its militaristic and aristocratic traditions. But precisely because of its codes of honour and decency – and a remarkably low rate of membership of the Nazi party – as well as its misguided belief in its own strength and independence, the army protested in the strongest terms, at least from the top. One member of the *Abwehr* (military intelligence), Hans Bernd Gisevius, an active anti-Nazi, declared that 'Not a single general had had the impulse to bring out his troops and see to the clearing of the streets. The army played deaf and blind. The meaning of this is clear.'[11] But it must be stressed that events began, simultaneously and all over Germany, at 3 in the morning. An army cannot mobilise at such short notice. And besides, go where? to every single town in the nation? Armies need organisation time and hundreds of signed forms before they can move. And barracks are not always sited near town centres. The next day it seemed as if the riots were over, and their resumption in the early afternoon again caught everybody by surprise.

As it was, senior army generals, among them Stulpnagel, von Hanneken and von Roth, demanded an audience with Hitler, who refused to see them.[12] Instead they told Göring that the persecutions of the Jews dishonoured Germany, and that Jewish people who wanted to should be allowed to leave Germany, and with their capital. It seemed this protest had had an effect when, on 21 November, Hitler ordered the release of several hundred Jews from Dachau. But it was only to catch off guard the generals, who were subsequently arrested for inciting unrest against the führer. And that was it for them.[13]

Kristallnacht immediately backfired on the Nazis in a manner that might be called poetic justice. We speak not of the international revulsion that was inevitably provoked, which deeply worried Hitler, and about which we will later hear much more. Instead there was the simple fact that the Nazis had broken billions of marks' worth of plate glass. This was equivalent to nearly the yearly output of the Belgian glass industry, which existed mainly to supply Germany. Very

well, one can do without glass for a time, but the Jewish shops –
often leased from German gentile landlords – were insured by and
large through German insurance firms, and were rarely re-insured
outside the country. To default on insurance claims would not only
effectively defraud German citizens, but would also smear
Germany's reputation for business in the international community.
The Nazis were faced with paying for Kristallnacht themselves, and
many within the party organisation were furious with Goebbels for
instigating the expensive riots. Walter Funk, the economics minister, was livid:

> Have you lost your head, Goebbels? How can you care to
> commit such base acts? It is a disgrace to be a German today!
> I knock myself out to preserve the economic solidity of the
> nation, and you throw millions out of windows. If you don't
> put a stop to this immediately, I will resign![14]

Göring, arguably the century's most duplicitous individual,
recounted his reactions to the riots at his trial after the war:

> I declared that I wanted no part of those methods. As the
> person responsible for the four-year plan, I was striving des-
> perately to obtain maximum results.
>   In several speeches, I had asked people to save even
> empty toothpaste tubes, and rusty bent screws, and to turn
> them over to the recycling centres. And in the space of only
> one night, millions and millions of marks' worth of mer-
> chandise were stupidly destroyed. Goebbels didn't care a fig
> for the economics of the situation.[15]

Both these quotes are noteworthy because they show – in the
case of Göring it was part of his attempt to escape the gallows – that
the Nazis were almost chemically incapable of feeling sympathy for
the Jews, or conceiving of them as fellow human beings. Every sentiment expressed merely concerns the economics of the matter.

The only Nazi to address his guilt and culpability (and this twenty years after) was Albert Speer, in his book, *Inside the Third Reich*:

> On November 10, driving to the office, I passed by the still smouldering ruins of the Berlin synagogues ... Today this memory is one of the most doleful of my life, chiefly because what most disturbed me was the aspect of disorder that I saw ... Most of all I was troubled by the political revival of the 'gutter'. The smashed panes of shop windows offended my sense of middle class order.[16]

It is stupifying that even here the Jews are not mentioned once. Speer's book is incredible because of its self-questioning and introspection, quite apart from the riveting detail he provides of life behind the scenes with Hitler. But all there was to offend him in Kristallnacht was the mess. At least he is honest about it. I can think of no other example in history where the saving human ability to put oneself in the other fellow's shoes has been so cauterised, removed almost surgically from the spirit, as in the Nazi machine.

It is vitally important to understand the prescience of Herschel's action in the light of this, and so in the end sympathise with him *despite* Kristallnacht. He was 'existentially' converted to personal war in the light of the Nazis' utter indifference to the humanity of the Jews. He saw this before anybody else, not intellectually but instinctively, and so saw what the Jews were up against. In other words he looked into the future, and his action wilfully provoked it. In doing so he created suffering for his people within Hitler's reach, but he saved more than that in the long-term, as we shall argue. Above all he succeeded in alerting the world to Nazism.

As postscript to the unmatched callousness there is the solution that Goebbels, Funk and Göring came up with to resolve the problem of all the breakages: make the Jews pay. Since Kristallnacht was clearly the fault of the Jews (one of whom on behalf of them all had assassinated etc etc), then it was their responsibility to make reparations to the German people. All insurance payments received by

Jews for damage to their property (which mounted to 600 million marks) were deemed fraudulent, and they were made to hand over the pay-outs to German authorities and repair the damage inflicted out of their own pockets.

They were to turn over all property salvaged from within damaged commercial premises to the government, which in addition levied fines and charges for such expenses as cleaning the streets after the riots. In 1935 the Nazis had tallied the worth of the capital held by German Jews. It was estimated at between 7 and 10 billion marks. A special Kristallnacht tax of 2 billion marks was now levied upon this fortune, which Göring did not feel was excessive (he boasted how he objected to Goebbel's original figure as way too high).[17]

These measures were bundled together in what the Nazis called the 'Penitence Law'. The financial extortions were the least of it. Kristallnacht had become one of those occasions where the victim comes to bear the brunt of the repressed guilt of the perpetrator. It was scapegoating with a new, industrial-scale twist. The Jews were ordered to hand over all their property to the Reich, and out of this they would be placed on a special living allowance. No arrangements were ever made for its distribution, needless to say. From the beginning of 1939 they were formally prohibited from what had so far been informally but effectively enforced: running any business or personal craft, or having any connection with one. Goebbels, who ran the equivalent of the Ministry of Heritage, declared that no Jews would be permitted to enter 'his' concert halls, movie houses, art galleries, theatres, swimming pools, or anything else. Jewish newspapers were banned and Jewish schools shut down. Jewish children in mixed schools were formally barred from attending.

All this new Jewish leisure-time was rigorously legislated over, as well.[18] There were rules about where Jews could go: if to a park, whether they were allowed to sit on a park bench, or if to a forest whether they could stray from the path. They were no longer allowed to drive or use public transport. The wearing of yellow stars was now compulsory. One could go on. All these were declared on 12 November, and Goebbels was quick to explain and justify:

> The murder of a German Diplomat was carried out to provoke trouble between Germany and other great European powers, thus troubling an international situation that had begun to improve. It was a shot in the back ... The Jew Grynszpan declared that he wished to hit at the German people through the intermediary of their government. The German people have now answered in like fashion.
>
> Under the measures decided yesterday, Jewish enterprises will completely disappear from German economic life, and will be transferred to Aryan owners ... Within the briefest possible period, the German nation will find a satisfactory solution to the Jewish question.[19]

It is not surprising that, in the face of such overwhelming and frightening reaction, both the French and German Jews quickly united in condemning Herschel. Britain and France also denounced the assassination – both were understandably wary of an unleashed Nazi rage. One Nazi *Gauleiter* had asked Churchill which of the German laws against Jews might cause problems between the two countries. Churchill replied none of them.[20] Such were the times.

Herschel, then, was isolated in more than one sense. Support would soon be winging its way from the States, and sections of French opinion would later rally. But a few days after vom Rath's death, it looked as though Herschel had single-handedly transformed himself into the Angel of Death for the German and Austrian Jews. It is easy to confuse the immediate effects of his crime with a judgment on it, as Cuenot was to do years later. But we should be aware – as is Schwab, who experienced Kristallnacht personally, and got out of Germany indirectly because of Herschel Grynszpan – that Herschel succeeded in alerting both the Reich's Jews and the world at large. He truly flushed out the Nazis. Goebbels, Hitler's

Rottweiler, was free to run, and he chased from Germany Jews who otherwise would have perished in concentration camps. As Schwab calculates, there was a net saving of lives directly attributable to Kristallnacht and the repressive measures that followed in its wake.

What is more, the Nazis had been prepared for what they did. The communication from Müller quoted above had been waiting in his desk drawer for months and was ready to send with few alterations. The Penitence Tax simply required an updated name, for it had been ready to be imposed for some time. And the 30,000 Jewish men carted off to concentration camps found that all was ready for them on their arrival. Schwab quotes a long-term political prisoner of Sachsenhausen, who worked there as a quartermaster, and who had shortly before Kristallnacht received orders to make ready a very large amount of new uniforms. There had also been supplies of yellow cloth delivered, bolts and bolts of it, for making the yellow stars. He was reprimanded when he went to put it into storage, and was told to supervise its cutting and stitching immediately. In other words, the whole thing was planned.[21] Indeed, Herschel may have saved the life of the German ambassador in Paris twice over. It is known that Hitler was ready to have his ambassador in Vienna, von Papen, murdered by the SD in order to provoke an invasion of Austria. Only the Austrians' sudden conversion to the idea of Anschlüss (after their leader, von Schusnigg, had visited Hitler at Berchtesgarten, and heard things straight from the horse's mouth) saved his neck.[22]

It is probable that Kristallnacht was going to happen within a week or two of 9 November in any case. An assassination of von Welczeck in Paris would have been the obvious provocation. That Herschel's crime had led to the consequences it did prompted many to speculate that he was a Nazi agent. If this was true it was only in the most unintentional way – and actually it was not true at all, as we hope to have made clear from showing exactly what happened. The arguments for Herschel the Nazi largely rest on his possession of the mythical 3,000 francs. He never had this money.[23]

Lastly, though, for all its planning, we should not fall into the trap of assuming that Kristallnacht was simply a calmly executed piece of political chicanery. It was also, and had to be, an ecstatic outburst, at least on the part of the Nazis who engaged in the destruction. Besides accomplishing political and material goals, they were satisfying some form of primal hunger, or desire, that made them so angry and ashamed that their scapegoating of its object (the Jews) reached unheard of proportions.

The last word in this chapter should go to an Englishman named Smallbones. He was a consul-general in Frankfurt-am-Main, and was in love with all things German except Nazism. He had lived there for years, and adored the place. The Foreign Office could not persuade him to take his leave. He was shocked into disbelief by what he saw on 9 and 10 November, and came to a stunning conclusion. He said that the riots were of the nature of 'sadistic cruelty' and that its origin was 'sexual perversion, and in particular homo-sexuality'. Today, we would of course say repressed homosexuality, manifested as homophobia, and disguised as hatred for its object of desire. 'It seems to me that mass sexual perversity may offer an explanation for this otherwise inexplicable outbreak' he went on.[24] Plainly an amateur Freudian, he is not a bad anthropologist, and these are amazing words to come from a Foreign Office employee in 1938. But I think he is right. Hitler's rabid aversion to homosexuality is well-documented, and was seen as a weakness at the time (British Intelligence planned to infiltrate the Chancellery and spray effeminate perfume about the place in an attempt to provoke a nervous breakdown in the führer).

But the Nazi attitude to the Jews is seen nowhere more clearly in this respect than in the rhetoric and the cartoons. First, as we have already noted, the Jews were seen as a sexual infection. There are many examples of innocent young fräuleins being caressed by older, ridiculously masculinised (hairy, big-nosed) Jewish men – daddy-figures without doubt. Behind this image promulgated by the Nazis is the childish assumption that the woman is not just being stolen, but that there is nothing to be done. The prevailing Nazi emotion seems to be a helpless, infantile rage, that secretly sees all women as mother-figures ready and willing to betray. A lethal self-pity. What is wanted is the power to win her back. The Nazis were fetishistic about power – witness the uniforms and insignia of rank they would regularly gather to admire, like a group of psychopathic trainspotters. The Nazis saw this power in the strong and patriarchal Jewish religion. It was the feared and strongly desired Father for them. I believe that what we see in Nazi ideology and in Kristallnacht in particular is on one level hysterical Oedipal rage, and a transmuted desire to 'fuck-to-death' the Jewish father. It is a dark and one-sided love affair the Nazis were pursuing with the Jews.[25]

Herschel's act was an unbearable provocation, and this psychobabble is important to stress now in the light of how strangely and how well the Nazis later treated him. In spite of their progressive demonisation of the Jews, all the evidence was to the contrary. The race was intelligent, sober, moral, thrifty and meek. In short, everything the Nazis hated, but maybe secretly envied as well. Finally to discover, in the slight person of Herschel Grynszpan, a Jew who was also daring, fearless and adept at violence was tantalising and unbearable. They finally had the demon figure they had fantasised about, and he became the Nazis' fetishized figure incarnate. It was bad news for the Jews on 9 November 1938, but it may well have saved Herschel's life.

CHAPTER SEVEN

DEATH AND DETENTION

There was chaos and panic in vom Rath's office. Those who quickly arrived on the scene included Ernst Achenbach, Count Welczeck's secretary, who managed to talk briefly with vom Rath. The wounded man claimed that Herschel had fired almost immediately upon entering the room,[1] although we *know* that Herschel was sitting down opposite the German for a few moments, working up the courage to pull out his gun. This is confirmed by the paths of the bullets once they had entered vom Rath's body. Both slugs travelled upwards, which means that vom Rath had sprang to his feet when he saw the gun and that Herschel was indeed seated. Thus we know for certain that vom Rath did not remain in his chair and then, once hit, slump over his desk as Read and Fisher claim. Also, their idea that Herschel had a pop-gun is refuted by the way that the bullets each travelled intact nearly twelve inches through tough skin, tissue, bone and internal organs. Why did vom Rath alter the details so? He repeated to Achenbach what Herschel had yelled at him, except that he left out the detail about the 'document'. Clearly vom Rath, though in trauma, was good enough at his (other) job to keep his wits about him. It is possible he was equally worried over what might be found in his desk drawer, or even on his blotter.

Kreuger and Nagorka, who held Herschel, reported the sequence of events to Autret, the gendarme Herschel had spoken with outside the embassy. Kreuger added that vom Rath still lived, to which Herschel responded, 'It's a shame that he isn't dead'.[2] The embassy physician, Dr Claas, had been called on the telephone and was rushing over. In the meantime, first aid was administered by Aschenbach and *Botschaftsrat* (Counsellor of Embassy) Brauer. Neither could cope with the massive hæmhorraging, though, which was serious because one of the bullets had passed through vom Rath's spleen, then his stomach, and finally lodged in the pancreas. There is not much more damage a single bullet can do in the mid-section of the body. The other bullet had entered vom Rath's left side as well, but slightly higher, had travelled relatively harmlessly through the chest cavity, missing the lungs, and had lodged in the right shoulder.[3]

Ambassador Welczeck was of course blissfully ignorant of what was taking place. It was said at the time that he was shaving, but had he been on the premises he would have heard the commotion and hurried along lathered or no. The tale related by Georges Bonnet, the French Foreign Minister is more believable. He said that Welczeck turned up at his office slightly after the shooting – in a lather all right – claiming that he had narrowly escaped an assassination attempt. In this he was correct. Only the fact that he was out on his morning constitutional (that, and his habit of not talking to strangers on the street) had saved his life. Herschel had not sought out vom Rath in particular. Any official would have sufficed, and the more senior the better. Bonnet was horrified, like the ambassador, not so much because vom Rath had been hurt, but because the delicate piecing together of a Franco-German friendship pact they had been working on could now be in jeopardy.

By now an ambulance had arrived at the embassy, and there was discussion over where to take vom Rath. The American hospital in Neuilly was better equipped and had a better reputation than the local French *clinique* (private hospital). But it was across town, and the bleeding was serious. It was decided to take vom Rath to the Alma Clinic at 166 rue de l'Université. Professor Baumgartner, a top French surgeon, was informed of the impending arrival, and was already scrubbed up when vom Rath was carried in. The wounded man went straight into emergency surgery: it was not just his life that was being saved but the diplomatic relationship between France and Germany. It was quickly dawning on everyone involved that they had a large-scale international incident on their hands.

The first thing the medics required was blood. These were the days before refrigerated blood-banks, and a donor was needed, lying down on a table right next to the recipient. Dr Jubé, a noted transfusion specialist, was on hand, together with Paris's premiere blood donor, one M Thomas. This was a man who gave blood away for Christmas and birthdays; who would give you his blood whether you wanted it or not. He was a veteran of the First World War, decorated with the Croix de Guerre and the Médaille Militaire, and now ran a restaurant, presumably to keep up his strength. He had given blood over 100 times since 1930, and arrived with considerable pomp to transfuse good-will into the Franco-German relationship. The newspapers lapped it up, as did the Nazi propagandists, who saw a Frenchman singlehandedly attempting to repair the damage inflicted upon the Fatherland by the Jewish race.

Baumgartner was in a sweat, working at lightning speed, his legendary hands a blur over vom Rath's damaged body. He ignored the second bullet for the time being and concentrated on the one lodged in the pancreas. He removed the spleen, stitched together the torn stomach and finally got to work on vom Rath's pancreas. The blood-clots were tweezered out, then the second bullet removed, and the patient sewn up. After that, the celebrity blood of M Thomas, *Hero de la République*, was pumped into the unconscious German.

The operation had gone smoothly. Vom Rath, though obviously still on the critical list, was hanging in. Baumgartner was customarily modest and sceptical. He shrugged his shoulders and said, 'If only there had been one wound, but there are three!' (i.e. not three bullets, but three injuries: pancreas, stomach and spleen). Cuenot adds that besides having no blood banks, the world had yet no anti-biotics and – more importantly – no anti-trypsiques, which are used to treat illnesses of the spleen. These last would not have helped had the pancreatic injury also included damage to the excretory canal.[4] But since Baumgartner did not mention it (three wounds not four) we must assume vom Rath's cloud had a silver lining.

By now the news had reached Germany. Hitler's response was immediate: he dispatched his own personal doctors, Brandt and Magnus, to Paris without delay. They boarded a Junkers transport in Berlin, stopped over at Cologne, and landed at Le Bourget just before dawn the next morning, checked into a flashy *rive droit* hotel, and arrived at the Alma Clinic at 10:30 a.m., 8 November. It was after this that vom Rath's condition began to deteriorate.

Vom Rath's brother, Gunther, and his distraught father, had travelled from Dusseldorf to Cologne, and from there had caught the night express train to Paris. They arrived at the clinic about the same time as Dr Magnus and Professor Brandt, and saw the stricken Ernst, who was of course still unconscious. Vom Rath's mother had delayed her departure to Paris by a little while so she could pack a suitcase. She was preparing for a bedside vigil. When she arrived the following morning she went with her husband and son to the clinic and found Ernst conscious but extremely weak. He was visibly delighted to see his family, but they told him not to try to speak.

At mid-day Brandt and Magnus rolled up in a limousine and disappeared inside to see the patient. They emerged with a grim message and were oddly fatalistic: 'We can say nothing except that the condition of the patient is still very grave and we will undoubtedly return during the course of the day.'[5] They disappeared for a leisurely lunch, and returned in the early afternoon, at which point vom Rath promptly sank into a diabetic coma brought about by the injury to the pancreas, which usually produces the insulin the body requires. It also produces the digestive enzymes that can dissolve the internal organs and kill with peritonitus, but that was not the problem in this case.

It was naturally a great honour to have the führer's personal physicians looking after your son, and even Baumgartner would have graciously given way to Brandt and Magnus. And what would they have done? One guesses they would have administered insulin. Perhaps they asked for insulin and witnesses saw them inject vom Rath. If it was insulin and not water, that is.

It should be crystal clear by now what is being suggested – and what a grave and heartless slur this is on two dedicated doctors. Dedicated to the führer, that is. Dedicated to the Final Solution, at least. The fact is, Herr Professor Brandt stood trial at Nuremburg, and was condemned to death and hung, for his enthusiastic and hands-on approach to cruel medical experiments performed on concentration camp inmates. There is no evidence that these two, one of them at least a devil, were any great upholders of the Hippocratic oath.[6]

On the other hand the evidence that they did away with vom Rath (it would not have taken much; it could have been done very subtly; a gentle nudge in the direction of death was all that was needed) is purely circumstantial. It is no certainty, except that it should be borne in mind what a disaster for Hitler it would have been had vom Rath survived. As we have seen, all the preparations were in place for Kristallnacht or something like it, and only a pretext to begin the pogrom was needed. Here, suddenly, was the perfect excuse offered up on a plate. A Jew had murdered a loyal German diplomat and a member of the Nazi Party to boot. It was proof positive of the Jewish conspiracy to destroy Germany and to destabilise international relations. The Nazis had an honest-to-God martyr on whose behalf they could teach the 'Jewish vermin' a lesson.

Imagine if vom Rath had survived. The Nazis would have been deprived of a martyr to begin with, and although Kristallnacht could still have been launched, it would not have appeared (at least to the Nazis) so perfectly justified or apt. What if vom Rath had survived and it transpired he was not such a red-hot Nazi as he had meanwhile been portrayed? That would have been embarrassing (and one can imagine vom Rath's file was on Hitler's desk the minute he heard of the shooting). Thirdly, November 9 was a mere 36 hours away when Hitler heard of the attack. If vom Rath was dead by then, the entire conjugation of events was almost supernaturally inspired (remember what a great believer Hitler was in heavenly alignments). Fourthly, vom Rath's desk would have been gone through by now. The embassy Gestapo would have had to report back to Berlin. If the hypothesis that vom Rath was working as an anti-Nazi agent is correct, then the Nazis could have figured it out by about the time Brandt and Magnus went into the hospital, and at about the time vom Rath lapsed into his coma. The day vom Rath was shot was the day, as we have noted, that he was due to hand over to the *Deuxième Bureau* the list of transmitter sites. It is possible this was found in his desk, and that he was a dead man, bullets or not, from that moment on.

Even if he was not a spy, though, it is clear that it was overwhelmingly in Hitler's interest for vom Rath to die. One thinks again of the narrowly avoided murder of von Papen in Vienna. Hitler had shown himself quite able to kill off his own loyal people when it suited him.

What is more, this was the second assassination of a German diplomat, and the one Hitler had fervently been hoping for. The first was in Switzerland in 1935, when Gustloff, another German diplomat, had been shot by a young Jewish man in a protest similar to Herschel's. But it was too early back then for the Nazis really to take advantage of the situation. By 1938 the anti-Jewish laws had widened and hardened, and the Nazi grip on the government and police was almost complete. Another such assassination and they could proceed against the Jews as desired. Hence the preparations. And hence the certainty of vom Rath not surviving his treatment. He died at just after 4 o'clock that afternoon.

For a few moments after he had fired the revolver, Herschel was as shocked as his victim. The embassy secretaries recall he was shaking like a jelly; but Herschel very quickly composed himself, as his body and mind synchronised in a realisation of what had been done, and could not be undone. After that Herschel may have remained terrified, but at least he appeared calm. This calmness, though often stretched to breaking point, would never through all the dark years ahead leave him again.

Immediately he had one fantastic stroke of luck, without which there might well have been not much story left to tell. François Autret, the mild-mannered gendarme who had been stationed in the embassy quadrangle, was the same man who arrested Herschel and took him into custody. Autret frisked the ridiculously undersized assailant to make sure the weapon was not still secreted about his person (nobody had yet noticed it lying in a corner of the room), and when he went to lead Herschel away by the arm, the latter said, 'Don't worry, I will come with you.' Herschel was quiet on the way up the street to precinct headquarters on the rue de Bourgogne, a mere 500 yards away, but for one short, declarative statement: 'I've just shot a man in his office. I do not regret it. I did it to avenge my parents who are miserable in Germany.'[7] It was as if Herschel was saying this as much for his own benefit as anyone else's, to clarify in his mind what he had done and why. His words contained an inaccuracy (his parents were of course in Poland – almost) as well as some touching understatement that attests to his continuing shock and confusion.

So why was Autret leading Herschel away such a tremendous stroke of luck? Because of this: had any of the embassy employees their wits about them, and were they any less distracted by the prostrate and bleeding figure of the much-liked vom Rath, they would

have known to ignore Herschel's demand that he be turned over
to the French authorities and insist he stay exactly where he was,
inside the German embassy and at least technically speaking on
German soil, for the purposes of apprehension, trial and judgment. The fact that he was led off to be arraigned at a French
police station effectively delivered the crime and all the judicial
post-mortem effects into the hands of French law. Since the
accused was read his rights on French soil, it was there he had to
be tried. That Herschel was not a French citizen was of no weight.
The Germans, if they felt like trying to extradite him (which they
certainly did) could not even make the case that Herschel was one
of theirs, since they had taken away his right even to enter
Germany, never mind let him live there. Recall that as he was of
Polish parentage, Herschel never had an entitlement to German
citizenship in the first place. In the earliest moments after vom
Rath had been shot, then, the course of the amazing events to follow was determined.[8] To Hitler's steaming frustration, there was
nothing he could do to lay his hands on Herschel, except to
invade France. Which of course he did, and then went looking for
the boy with a vengeance. But until that point, the legal circus was
on.

After Autret handed Herschel over to the desk sergeant, the
young assassin was asked to turn out his pockets – which held some
loose change, his wallet containing the remaining banknotes, the
postcard avowing his intent to do something drastic that stupidly
he had forgotten to post (or was it that until the crucial moment
he was still undecided about his course of action?), a document
attesting that he had resided at 8 rue Martel (bad news for uncle
Abraham and aunt Chawa), the postcard he had received from
Berta in Zbaszyn, three invitations to a dance at *l'Aurore*, and the
registration form for his revolver. He had not filled it in, needless
to say. Perhaps it is because these small and irrelevant items gesture towards another life which has just been irrevocably closed
off, that they are so touching.

After that, deprived of his few personal effects, Herschel was briskly led away to be questioned. He would be interrogated twice during the day of 7 November, and before two separate police commissioners. The first was called Monneret, and Herschel straightaway began to unburden himself to the understanding cop. But in doing so he created problems later on. For example, Herschel's first description of the events in vom Rath's office did not include the provocation he was supposedly supplied with by the German: there was no mention of the 'dirty Jew' slur. If he had wanted to lessen his crime even a little (and it would have been a very little), that claim should have been put in at the first. What was worse was that, without really thinking what he was saying, Herschel referred in the most explicit terms to the postcard that Berta had sent:

> I received the postcard from my sister which was found in my wallet on Thursday November 3. It was from that moment on that I decided that as a means of protest I would kill a member of the Embassy.[9]

Those in the room looked at each other and shook their heads, not at the gravity of the crime but at the fact that Herschel was digging a deep hole for himself. As he had no lawyer present to advise him and tell him to shut his big mouth, Herschel simply carried on, eager to get things off his chest but closing off lines of defence in the process. It was only later that he would learn to dissemble effectively, and would also attempt to destroy the significance of the interrogation. He did this firstly by claiming he was beaten up by the police (probably untrue), and secondly by arguing that all he had said was inadmissible as evidence because he had no lawyer present (true, but hardly enforceable given the political pressures surrounding the case).

At the time, as if to compound his admission of intent, Herschel even offered, 'I aimed at the middle of the body'.[10] But he did not dream at this time of putting a name to the body, and the reason for this was very simple: he had absolutely no idea who he had killed. Herschel had never met vom Rath in his life. This seems a simple and banal point to highlight now, but it was extremely important and hotly debated in the light of Herschel's later accusations. The one matter that was really playing on his mind was the danger in which he had placed Abraham and Chawa.

If Herschel was careless about the rest of the information he supplied on the afternoon of 7 November, he made sure to protect as best he could his poor Parisian relatives. It didn't work. Herschel's first, hopeless gambit was to try to hide the fact that his residence and identity papers were all useless. Some time early on he realised the game was up on that score, so he said that he had left his aunt and uncle on 11 August and returned to Belgium to hide out. This three month fugitive interlude away from Paris was apparently underwritten by 3,000 Francs given to him by Abraham. Herschel did not stand by that detail for very long, though, and almost immediately admitted the cash had come from his father in Hanover. This was clearly a lie, since it was impossible to export money from Germany, especially for Jews and especially by wire or post.[11] Hidden in one's boot was the best bet, but nobody had come over to visit from Germany, as a quick check with the consulate would confirm. It was another appearance of the mythical 3,000 Francs, and another refutation of the theory that Herschel had been funded by the Nazis. This idea was popular with the French press, reflecting the anxiety of a readership that desperately desired to be exonerated from any political ramifications. As it was, the French police were already on their way to arrest Abraham and Chawa at their new address. The charge was to be harbouring an illegal alien.

This interrogation was the kind of scenario a policeman dreams about, and Monneret was having such an enjoyable and productive time that he allowed the questioning to continue until 5 o'clock in the afternoon. After that, Herschel was allowed to go and lie down in one of the cells, but he did not sleep. Already his mind was catching up with his mouth, and by the time he was led out not long before midnight for his second interrogation (with a new commissioner, Badin) he had started to get his story together.

Herschel had turned events over in his mind and decided he was unlikely to win any friends by appearing to be the aggressor. So, regardless of revolver and malice aforethought, he attempted to redraw his brief interview in vom Rath's office in a way that presented him more as the wounded party. It was sheer gall, but who in Herschel's position would not try such a tactic? He would not dream of denying his crime – the whole point was to be caught so an effective protest could be made – but he attenuated the impression that he was a ruthless murderer. The context in which he acted was begun to be made clearer:

> The official in question asked me to present the papers which
> I indicated I had. I then took out my revolver from my suit
> coat pocket and before firing I said, 'Isn't it enough that Jews
> have to suffer so severely from German persecution, and that
> they are thrown into concentration camps? Now they're being
> expelled as if they were nothing but stray dogs.'[12]

It is certainly an eloquent speech, though slightly less believable than his reported explanation, 'You're a filthy German and in the name of 12,000 persecuted Jews, here is the document!' But Herschel held firm. From this point on he flatly denied he used the expression, 'sale boche'. The boy was learning fast, and becoming slippery. Three weeks later, on November 29, he even went so far as to contradict his wild speech of the first interrogation (he had talked with the best lawyer in France during the interim). To the examining magistrate, Tesnière, Herschel declared, 'I did not really take aim. I fired aimlessly. It was the first time I had handled a firearm.'[13] The fact that most of the bullets went wide luckily served to lend weight to this claim.

Appearing before Badin on the night of the shooting, Herschel presented a further refinement of his drafting of the incident. Not only had vom Rath (still for Herschel at this time 'the official in question') insulted him, but he had managed to land a punch as well. Herschel's description of this incident did not help him though, since it made clear that the insult was delivered only after vom Rath had had two bullets pumped into him ('Wounded by the bullets, the official put both hands on his abdomen, and he still had the strength to give me a punch on the jaw calling me, at the same time, "dirty Jew"')[14]. As this indeed lessened the gravity and provocative power of the insult, Herschel duly amended his story once again on 19 December, and said he couldn't remember if 'dirty Jew' came before or after he fired.[15] I do not think the insult was ever delivered, for reasons already discussed. What is more, Herschel awarded himself the honour of having warned vom Rath to defend himself before he drew his gun, and credited the gravely wounded man with an ability to supply not just one punch, but a whole barrage of right and left hooks. At this rate, Herschel was likely to end by being the victim of an evil vom Rath, and this indeed was how his story wound up. But that would be in 1942, a long way down a winding road.

Almost immediately after he died, Ernst vom Rath was lifted from his deathbed and wheeled to the clinic mortuary, where a famous Parisian pathologist, Dr Paul, performed an autopsy. Nothing that was not already known was revealed. The fatal bullet was, as expected, pronounced to be the fatal bullet. Indeed, because it was so expected, it is not clear that the pathologist went looking for anything else, like strange substances in the veins. Not that he would have found anything, it being a lack rather than a surplus of chemicals that would have been deadly. Brandt and Magnus were naturally on hand to reassure the Frenchman had he any doubts, and to hurry him along. They drafted the announcement of vom Rath's demise to the ranks of pressmen waiting outside, and it underlined the pancreatic orthodoxy, as it were.

> The first secretary of the Embassy Ernst vom Rath died fol-
> lowing wounds which he received on November 7. During the
> course of the morning of November 9, his condition worsened
> in spite of the inoculations and the fever remained high.
> Towards mid-day the effect of the stomach injury became
> more evident and the strength of the patient began to ebb.[16]

It was a straightforward statement, except for the fact that vom
Rath's condition did not worsen until the afternoon of the 9th, when
Brandt and Magnus got their hands on him. During the morning
he had been delighted to see his family, and the fever was in check
at least enough for him to appear lucid. Interesting, too, that the
German doctors felt a need to refer to the ineffectiveness of certain
'inoculations' (perhaps a small dose of disavowal there?), and even
the normally trusting Cuenot was led to add that, 'To forestall any
other interpretations, the doctors concluded by attesting that vom
Rath succumbed due to the seriousness of the wounds, which was
plainly evident. This precaution did not hinder certain suspicious
souls, however, from thinking that Hitler had sent his two doctors
to finish off what his assassin had failed to do.'[17] Cuenot is uninterested in following up this line of investigation, and on the whole
is amazingly trusting of the Nazis, bestowing on their claims and
actions a transparency history would blink at. One does not need to
be a conspiracy theorist to add up the facts and circumstances and
be left with an odd, fish-like smell.

At 10:30 in the evening, vom Rath's body was removed to a chapel
on nearby rue de Lille, and all night long Embassy staff held a vigil.
Of all the lengthy and overblown funeral arrangements to come, this
was certainly the most genuine gesture. Already vom Rath's posthumous humiliations had begun, though, with a huge swastika draped
over the coffin. The Nazi state was claiming his body as its own property for propaganda purposes, and his grieving family was forced to
concur.

It would take over a week before poor vom Rath was laid in the ground, and when he was moved to the German Lutheran church on Sunday 12th, it was just the beginning of his homeward odyssey to the family plot in Düsseldorf. Various French and German governmental representatives attended the service held at the church on rue Blanche, and Secretary of State Baron von Weizsaker, as Hitler's representative, delivered a speech. It was foggy dawn on Wednesday 16th before a specially chartered train crawled over the border into the Fatherland at a suitably funereal pace. Aboard, in addition to a full complement of journalists, were von Weizsaker, von Welczeck, and Herr Professor (of Law) Freidrich Grimm, from whom we will soon be hearing much more.

The railroad bier made its stately way through Germany at 12 miles an hour, with people thronging along the length of its route. The journey terminated in Düsseldorf, where the coffin was laid in state at the planetarium (of all places). For the next 24 hours, lines of silent and melancholy Germans shuffled past the body of the obscure young ex-diplomat. At noon on Thursday the funeral itself took place. This is the most interesting incident in the ironical and overblown return of a brave young anti-Nazi tragically wounded by a boy with whom he may well have been privately in sympathy, and neatly finished off by his Nazi enemies. Whether they were aware of what vom Rath was up to or not, he was certain to make a much greater contribution to the *kampf* on his back in the planetarium than in his office in Paris.

Hitler himself arrived promptly to take part in the ceremony. An accomplished ham actor, he made sure that he was unannounced by either fanfares or tribunes. Thus, his silently dramatic entrance even more attracted the attention of those in attendance. He strode over to the rows of seats, and placed himself in the empty chair between vom Rath's mother and father. And he did not say a word to them. And he did not contribute at all to the speeches delivered, which were left to Secretary of State Bohle and Foreign Minister von Ribbentrop. The orations were entirely predictable: propagandist exhortations over the corpse of vom Rath and a few other Germans who had perished abroad (the fact that most of these were in combat, helping the fascists in the Spanish Civil War, seemed not to lessen the tone of petulance and outrage).[18] Von Ribbentrop, a foolish man, and one of Hitler's puppets who could be trusted to pull his own strings,[19] delivered the most typical example of Nazi thinking:

> The entire German nation is in mourning. A hostile world, rigid in its outmoded structure, thinks it can prevent her forward stride. Lies, calumny, terror and assassination are the means by which international Jewry hopes to bar the future progress of Nazi Germany. German and French medical skill, the comradeship of a French war veteran have proven to be in vain. On November 9, comrade vom Rath closed his eyes in eternal sleep. Party comrade, now you can sleep in peace! Slowly but surely the old world is crumbling. No terror exists which can stop the rise of Germany. If today, a new wave of hate breaks out against us, if once again there is an attempt to profane the memory of our dead, then a storm of indignation will sweep across Germany. As a result, the will of the people will be further strengthened. We have understood the challenge and will know how to answer it.[20]

Hitler departed as soon as the National anthem had played, with barely a nod to the vom Raths. His behaviour was commented on, and while it is certain he had to run off in order to organise Nazi Day feastings in Bavaria (and of course the Kristallnacht agenda), the snub given to the family of the dead diplomat cannot pass unremarked. I think the reasons for Hitler's odd behaviour are two-fold. In the first place, he wanted his silence to be noteworthy, as its purpose was to communicate the depth of his anger: he was to appear, quite literally, speechless with rage. Secondly, and this is related to the way the vom Raths were cashiered into letting their son's burial be so wantonly hijacked (neither of Ernst's parents were Nazis

– quite the contrary – and they wanted a quiet, private ceremony), I think Hitler was aware by this point of just who and what vom Rath was. His relationship *vis-à-vis* French intelligence could well have been discovered, as we noted, and Hitler was allowing his anger at vom Rath be construed by witnesses as anger against the Jewish assassin. It would be quite typical for Hitler's mind to work this way, and to capitalise on his outrage by threatening the family what would happen if they did not let their son's funeral turn into a Party rally. One remembers the way in which, after the army plotters against Hitler's life were executed by firing squad, their widows were presented with an invoice for the price of the bullets. In such a fashion was Hitler apt to use his anger further to degrade and humiliate his victims.

Ernst vom Rath was laid to rest in the nearby family vault. *Requiescant in pace.*

CHAPTER EIGHT

DOROTHY AND VINCENT

The next morning, 8 November, Herschel was brought to be formally arraigned before the examining magistrate. The public prosecutor, Frette-Damicourt, had chosen to appoint Maître Jean Tesnière to this position. Such a decision showed both wisdom and understanding, for Tesnière was widely experienced in cases involving minors. He also had, let us say, political sensitivity. This was no crusading jurist, and could be trusted by the French authorities not to set about annoying the forces arrayed behind the plaintiff, namely Nazi Germany. This awareness of the French situation *vis-à-vis* its threatening and aggressive neighbour would have detrimental effects on the fortunes of the defence, though. Cuenot is keen to point out that Tesnière was 'esteemed in his profession for qualities of intelligence, independence, integrity, finesse and authority',[1] although Schwab is much less impressed by the man, and sees him as a willing co-operator with the Nazis and their representatives in the period of the pre-trial investigation.

I think both commentators are correct in their opinions, which is to say that Tesnière's usually sterling talents and qualities were necessarily blunted (on Ministry of Justice – which in this case meant Presidential -- orders) due to the precarious international situation and the obvious flashpoints that could be lit up by the progress and conclusion of Herschel's case. Tesnière need not have been a Nazi sympathiser to have looked as if he were one, given the context of the trial and the demands made on him by his alarmed government.

Tiny Herschel was flanked by three of the heaviest and most ugly detectives in the Paris Sûreté – slight overkill, perhaps, but a tacit message to the Nazis that the French were taking this business seriously. In the intervening twenty-four hours, uncle Abraham had not been idle. He had secured for Herschel the services of the 'family lawyers', Monsieurs Szwarc and Vésinne-Larue. They were neighbourhood attorneys, obvious choices for a poor Jew in trouble, and were eminently agreeable to Herschel, since they were of his culture, and he could speak to them in Yiddish. The only problem was that they had never handled a case of such import, with so many international and political dimensions, and with such publicity. Though Szwarc and Vésinne-Larue were eager to defend Herschel, and were looking forward to basking in the glory of the headlines and to their enhanced reputations, it was plain they were well out of their depth.

Tesnière straightaway asked Herschel to fill in everybody on the reasons for his actions, to give a background and perspective to the violence. Luckily, with Herschel speaking French but poorly, Tesnière was able to help out the young defendant by translating his words from the German. Herschel proceeded to deliver a modest and moving speech, which he had obviously been refining in his mind overnight, and which was reported by *Le Temps* the next day as follows:

> The Jewish race has a right to live, and I do not understand all the sufferings that the Germans are inflicting upon them. If you are a Jew you can obtain nothing, attempt nothing, and hope for nothing. You are hunted like an animal. Why this martyrdom?

It was not with hatred or for vengeance that I acted, but because of love for my parents and for my people who were subjected unjustly to outrageous treatment. Nevertheless, this act was distasteful to me and I deeply regret it. However, I had no other means of demonstrating my feelings. It was the constantly gnawing idea of the suffering of my race which dominated me. For 28 years my parents resided in Hanover. They had set up a modest business which was destroyed overnight. They were stripped of everything and expelled. It is not, after all, a crime to be Jewish. I am not a dog. I have the right to live. My people have a right to live on this earth.[2]

The questioning went on all day long, finally drawing to a close at 5:30 p.m. Herschel repeated all he had said the day before, this time adding the 'filthy Jew' slur that vom Rath had supposedly hurled at him. Afterwards he was taken to Fresnes prison. This was no great ordeal because Fresnes was no Bastille. Surprisingly for the 1930s, it was a most enlightened penal institution, specifically set up to house youngsters, and seemingly designed by a benevolent social worker. There was a good deal of freedom for the inmates, who were allowed access to books and newsprint. The food was excellent, the building of ultra-modern design, light and airy.[3] There were single cells, and ample supplies of pens and paper, for the prisoners were encouraged to note down all their thoughts in the form of a diary. Needless to say, precocious Herschel speedily filled two entire volumes. His words were, of course, used by the authorities as it pleased them.

At this time the crime, though a serious one of attempted murder, had not yet turned into a full-scale murder investigation. Vom Rath, on 8 November, was making fair progress in hospital. There was a lingering chance that everything might blow over, and the French were hoping all could be contained. The next afternoon changed all that, though, and the reports and examinations increased many fold in their depth and complexity. After vom Rath died, the French knew they were in a political pickle.

The next day, after the Kristallnacht pogrom had begun in Germany, the true extent of the nightmare was revealed. Little comfort could be taken by the French government in the knowledge that Herschel was a foreigner. Although the Nazis could not be angry with the French for the crime itself, there would be great mischief if Herschel was not seen in Germany to have been punished sufficiently by the French; nay, with exemplary harshness. In 1938 it would have been both easy and convenient for Herschel quickly to have been found guilty. French public opinion would have been placated, since it was no great lover of Jews, and resented the potential damage done to Franco-German accord. Also Jewish opinion, in the aftermath of Kristallnacht, held no sympathy at all for Herschel. It was more concerned with the plight of the 400,000 Jews effectively held hostage within Hitler's Reich.

Tesnière's strategy of choice, given the limited international space within which he had to manœuvre, was strictly to ignore every circumstance preceding the crime itself. In legal terms he was being permissibly strict, and politically he was pleasing both his French paymasters and his German pressurizers. These last were overjoyed by the fact that the judge of the case was apparently uninterested in what provoked Herschel to kill vom Rath. The Nazis would thus be able (without in open court having to defend themselves against their treatment of the Jews) candidly to submit their story of a worldwide Jewish conspiracy against the Fatherland, with Herschel making a star appearance as Tip of the Iceberg. It is easy to see how, practically in a strait-jacket, Tesnière came across as prejudiced against the defendant. In fact he was a loyal and patriotic Frenchman, and his prejudice was merely a reflection of the national policy and attitude.

If the attack on vom Rath made the front pages of the world press on 8 November, it was not with banner headlines. All this changed completely a couple of days later, though, when Kristallnacht unleashed a wave of journalistic revulsion unprecedented in its unanimity. The British papers intoned somewhat self-righteously, considering the fact that Britain was not giving the Jews much help, that Germany had returned to the Dark Ages. The London *Times* declared that, 'No foreign propagandist bent upon blaspheming Germany before the world could outdo the tale of burnings and beatings, of blackguardly assaults upon defenseless and innocent people'.[4] Even the *Daily Telegraph,* which supported Prime Minister Chamberlain's weak-kneed policy of endless appeasement, came out stiffly against the Nazis, saying, 'Germany has delivered herself over to an orgy of savagery which will send a thrill of horror through the civilised world.'[5]

It was in the United States, though, that the truest tones of outrage could be discerned. From Baltimore to Buffalo, from Omaha to San Francisco and all points between, America had its say. Union members instantly agreed to tithe part of their earnings to the victims of the Nazi atrocities, and schoolchildren took up collections from amongst their classmates. From Madison Square Garden ex-president Hoover, New York DA Thomas E Dewey, and former New York governor Alfred E Smith, all made radio broadcasts.[6] The most important and widely received transmission – and a mere taster of the kind of help and support for the Jews, and for Herschel in particular, that was to come from her – was made by a journalist named Dorothy Thompson.

In fact, to call Dorothy Thompson a journalist seems somehow inadequate. A journalist she was for sure, this sparkling and charismatic woman, syndicated nationwide and with a by-line readership of over ten million by the end of the nineteen-thirties. But she was also the Second Lady of the United States, and that when there was stiff competition for the title. Dorothy was a New England preacher's daughter, that irrepressible breed, who had vaguely, in a late nineteenth-century fashion, harboured a desire to be a writer. To her this meant sub-sub-Emily Dickinson poetry and romantic novels, until her father told Dorothy to go and see some life. She fetched up as a volunteer in the women's suffrage headquarters in

New York, and the experience transformed her from a dreamy fictionalist into a tough and campaigning realist.

Dorothy became not a feminist but a liberated woman, taking her right to equality in her stride and not normally even bothering to rehearse her arguments to the patronising and condescending men around her. But when she did, she was withering. Dorothy was of that generation and stock through which American womanhood bloomed into independence, autonomy and public life, in a way unimaginable to their mothers. By the end of the First World War Dorothy was well into her career as a journalist, and soon found herself in Europe. By chance she wound up as a correspondent on Jewish affairs (these were the days when the Zionist State was being mooted), and as a stringer on this and other subjects so impressed herself upon the editors back in New York that they thought to save some money by putting her on salary. Soon, Dorothy was the first woman foreign correspondent, responsible for almost the whole of Eastern Central Europe, which included Austria, Czechoslovakia, Hungary and Romania, with her territory stretching as far east as Greece and Turkey.

Dorothy soon became thoroughly Europeanised, living first in Vienna (and growing fluent in German), then moving to Budapest, her favourite city of all, where she met and married Joseph Bard, a languorous Hungarian aristocrat and intellectual who, like a refugee from a Chekhov play, would forever be writing his unfinishable work, in four languages, on the European mind. Eventually they divorced and Dorothy, against her instincts and preferences, returned to the United States, where she embarked on a semi-disastrous marriage to one of the most widely read writers of the time, Sinclair 'Red' Lewis. Like many women of her generation, Dorothy was caught between the old feminine feeling of motherly responsibility for men, and the new, individualistic imperative to follow her own life and career.

Perhaps partly to assuage the guilt of an incomplete feminist evolution within herself, she chose for husbands men who more than most needed mothering, and who appealed to her tenderness by idolising her as a source of natural fecundity. It supplied Dorothy with a reassuring image of herself that she feared as a woman in a man's world she was losing. But it meant she was given hell by her men. Bard was the dreamy and demanding boy-child who suffocated Dorothy and denied her space of her own, and Lewis was a hopeless and emotionally violent alcoholic, competing with and blackmailing her so Dorothy would feel guilt over her 'selfish' career.

Above all, though, and most importantly for our story, Dorothy Thompson was the most vocal American anti-Nazi of her day. Her acquaintance with the object of her informed hatred had begun as far back as 1931, when she was living in Vienna again, after her Hungarian romance. Upon hearing Goebbels ranting about Nazism, she summed up his speech as propounding 'a peculiar mixture of Nordic myth, anti-semitism, militaristic tradition, desperado nationalism and moronised socialism'.[7] About the Nazi party's finest troops, the SS, she was characteristically blunt and perceptive: she thought they were 'pink-cheeked mediocrities' and 'a lot of wavy-haired bugger-boys'.[8] It was particularly sharp of her to see so early on, in the energies and outlook of the Nazis a load of repressed, or not so repressed, homo-eroticism, and this is more evidence to support our theory outlined above concerning the scapegoating of the Jews. But always, despite seeing them as ridiculous, she took Hitler and the Nazis very seriously indeed. The führer himself she called 'the perverter of Nietszsche' (Hitler for Dorothy was always above everything a pervert), and she described his philosophy with a concision that has yet to be bettered:

> Nazism is a repudiation of the whole past of western man. It is ... a complete break with Reason, with Humanism, and with the Christian ethics that are at the basis of liberalism and democracy ... In its joyful destruction of all previous standards; in its wild affirmation of the 'Drive of the Will'; in its Oriental

acceptance of death as the fecundator of life and of the will to death as the true heroism, it is darkly nihilistic. Placing will above reason; the ideal over reality; appealing, unremittingly, to totem and taboo; elevating tribal fetishes; subjugating and destroying the common sense that grows out of human experience; of an oceanic boundlessness, Nazism – that has been my consistent conviction – is the enemy of whatever is sunny, reasonable, pragmatic, common-sense, freedom loving, life affirming, form-seeking and conscious of tradition.'9

Strangely enough, Hitler was impressed by Dorothy Thompson and keen to meet her, and it is maybe for the devastating account of Hitler she set down after their meeting that Dorothy is best remembered. Why on earth Hitler wanted to lay himself open personally before one of his greatest detractors seems hard to imagine at first, until one remembers (as Speer describes) Hitler's appalling vanity, and the way in which he imagined his presence could affect people, especially women. And indeed it could, if they only adored and idolised the führer in the first place. But Adolf Hitler (née Schickelgruber) was mistaken in thinking he could charm Dorothy Thompson:

> When finally I walked into Adolf Hitler's salon in the Kaiserhof Hotel, I was convinced I was meeting the future dictator of Germany. In something less than fifty seconds, I was quite sure I was not. It took just about that time to measure the startling insignificance of this man who has set the world agog. He is formless, almost faceless, a man whose countenance is a caricature, a man whose framework seems cartilaginous, without bones. He is inconsequent and voluble, ill-poised, insecure. He is the very prototype of the little man.
>
> The eyes alone are notable. Dark gray and hyperthyroid – they have the peculiar shine which often distinguishes geniuses, alcoholics and hysterics. There is something irritatingly refined about him. I bet he crooks his little finger when he drinks his tea. His is an actor's face. Capable of being pushed out or in, expanded or contracted at will, in order to register facile emotions.10

Dorothy suffered from a degree of ridicule later in the decade, when her colleagues pointed out how wrong she had been. But in essence she was perfectly correct. She captures wonderfully Hitler's essential vulgarity: both his folk-pantomime repertoire of crude sentimentality, the ham actor's groundling appeal, and his petit-bourgeois pretentiousness – the idea of an oleaginous nobody attempting to be a leader not just of an empire, but more importantly of polite society ('I bet he crooks his little finger when he drinks his tea'). Hitler was certainly a paradox, a masterful leader to the Germans yet a joke and a clown to the rest of the world. The important thing to understand is how devastated and humiliated Germany had been after the end of the First World War. Hitler's apotheosis of the 'little man' into a figure of international stature was designed to restore dignity to the Germans, and it did. What Hitler looked like to foreigners was secondary to how he appeared to his countrymen. To them, the attitude of wounded dignity, and the solemnly absurd love of formality, though objectively ridiculous, made Hitler an object of adoration to them. And in the end it is not funny – Hitler was not funny – at all. For the world's laughter made it take the führer less seriously than it should have done.

It took another two years, before Dorothy was expelled for good from Germany, and the Gestapo were very polite about it, giving her 24 hours to leave before a formal notice of expulsion was served. [11] But Dorothy managed to get in one more dig at the Nazis even as her train was pulling out of the station:

> As far as I can see, I really was put out of Germany for the crime of blasphemy. My offense was to think that Hitler was just an ordinary man, after all. That is a crime against the reigning cult in Germany, which says that Mr Hitler is a messiah sent by God to save the German people – an old Jewish idea.[12]

It should be plain by now that feisty Dorothy, just like Hitler, was waiting for Herschel to happen: his crime fitted perfectly with her sense of duty and politics. The assassination and pogrom concretised all her warnings, and let her find an even more penetrating voice with which to berate not just the Nazis but also the free world. What she really had in common with Herschel, though, and what secretly galvanised her into activity on his behalf, was that Dorothy felt Herschel, like herself, knew something that nobody else had yet cottoned on to: that Germany was *already* at war, and the only thing to be done was fight tooth and nail against the Nazis, right now. 'Germany has gone to war already, and the rest of the world does not believe it',[13] she wrote as far back as 1934. And after the Anschluss Dorothy was convinced of what was to come:

> Write it down. On Saturday, February 12, 1938, military bolshevism, paganism and despotism started on the march across all of Europe east of the Rhine. Write it down that the world revolution began in earnest – and the world war.[14]

Dorothy watched aghast from New York as Kristallnacht broke over Germany. Her heart went out not just to Herschel but to all the Jews imprisoned within Hitler's Reich, and in an impassioned nationwide radio broadcast on the evening of 15 November, Dorothy told Herschel's story and appealed, beyond America, to the world:

> I am speaking of this boy. Soon he will go on trial. The news is that on top of all this terror, this horror, one more must pay. They say he will go to the guillotine, without a trial by jury, without the rights that any common murderer has ...
>
> Who is on trial in this case? I say we are all on trial. I say the Christian world is on trial. I say the men of Munich are on trial, who signed a pact without one word of protection for helpless minorities. Whether Herschel Grynszpan lives or not won't matter much to Herschel. He was prepared to die when he fired those shots. His young life was already ruined. Since then his heart has been broken into bits by the results of his deed.

They say a man is entitled to trial by a jury of his peers, and a man's kinsmen rally around him, when he is in trouble. But no kinsman of Herschel's can defend him. The Nazi government has announced that if any Jews, anywhere in the world, protest at anything that is happening, further oppressive measures will be taken. They are holding every Jew in Germany as a hostage.

Therefore, we who are not Jews must speak, speak our sorrow and indignation and disgust in so many voices that they will be heard. This boy has become a symbol, and the responsibility for his deed must be shared by those who caused it.[15]

To her frank surprise, the response to Dorothy's broadcast was overwhelming. Suddenly telegrams and sacks full of letters of support began to arrive, along with many cheques and bundles of cash she had not dreamed of asking for. The very next day, Dorothy announced that she was instituting the Journalists' Defence Fund to aid Herschel, and added as a proviso that, because of Hitler's threats, contributions should come only from non-Jews. It was a typically bold and unbuttoned American-style response to foreign maniacs, and there was a tradition of anti-fascist action, especially in New York, upon which Dorothy could call.

There is a story, for example, that at the end of the nineteenth century a mad anti-semitic preacher had arrived from Germany to spread his gospel of hate in the land of free-speech. When he disembarked in New York, he found that the mayor had assembled a forty strong police bodyguard to flank him wherever he went. The papers and hence the entire population were well aware that all of the bodyguard was Jewish, and the visiting preacher's tour was laughed to oblivion. Now, in 1938, the legendary Fiorello H La Guardia, the current mayor of New York, did exactly the same for the German Consulate General. A squad of burly Jewish cops, led by one Captain Max Finkelstein, now went everywhere the diplomat did, and that meant absolutely everywhere.[16] It should be mentioned, though, that despite the support for the Jews from the

American people, its government was not much more lax than the British and French when it came to allowing the desperate Jews to immigrate.

Dorothy immediately set about using some of the $40,000 the Fund smartly accrued to find a lawyer, a good lawyer, for Herschel. Meanwhile on the other side of the Atlantic, that was exactly what Herschel's family were about, too. There were, needless to say, big problems for the Parisian Grynszpans and Berenbaums (Chawa's family). Foremost among these was that, as soon as Herschel had been taken into custody and his garret on rue Martel turned upside down by the police, uncle Abraham and aunt Chawa had also been detained. As they were Herschel's legal guardians, the head of his defence organisation was, if not cut off, then whiplashed and temporarily disabled. A family council among those still at liberty was speedily convened, and the man who elected himself to take over was Salomon, Abraham and Sendel's other brother, and the one Abraham was none too fond of. Reading between the lines of bald fact, it seems that he was a little over eager in most things, a bit of a busybody, and frankly something of a pain in the rear end. Still, on this occasion he was doing the best he could, even if it was obvious he was sprinting for the limelight, perhaps blinded by it to the true extent of seriousness and danger lurking in the shadows.

He, together with Abraham Berenbaum (Chawa's brother), and Chawa's brother-in-law Jacques Wykhodz, saw all too clearly that Szwarc and Vésinne-Larue were not up to the task of handling a major murder trial in which the fate of millions of Jews was, to some undetermined extent, bound up. Thus, on 14 November they all trooped off to see Herschel in Fresnes prison and plead with him to allow a change of lawyers. It was not to be an easy task, for two reasons. First, Herschel had quickly become intimate and trusting with the two attorneys he already had: they could speak in Yiddish and not be understood by the Frenchmen around them, after all. The family was now suggesting that in addition to dispensing with these trusted professionals, a non-Jewish Frenchman should be engaged.

In the States, Dorothy's long range search for a top lawyer had borne fruit. There was one man who fitted her requirements perfectly in that he was second-to-none in the legal field in France, and not a Jew. In fact he was Catholic. And it was no coincidence that the name she had found was exactly that which, with trepidation, Herschel's relatives announced as they sat opposite him in the visiting room at Fresnes. And what was the name of this man whose reputation spanned two continents, this modern day Danton? He was Maître Vincent de Moro-Giafferi.

The Nazis had got there first, asking him, as their natural preference, to represent the family of vom Rath. Giafferi threw them out of his office. Apart from Dorothy Thompson, nobody hated and was more active against the Nazis than himself. Why then did they even ask him? The answer is simple enough: the Nazis assumed he was a lawyer like any other, which is to say they assumed he could be hired if the price was right. But Giafferi was not just another lawyer, and that fact was the key to his personality, and his phenomenal success.

Vincent de Moro-Giafferi was French, but more importantly he was Corsican, from the island which, like Sicily, still retained its ancient sense of tribalism and primitive hardness. Even today outlaws haunt its mountain-tops and caves, and the fierce singularity of Etruscan, perhaps even Mycenean blood, decreed that the Corsicans bowed to no man. Mysterious and insular, with an almost primeval sense of honour and determination, the Corsicans looked on the sophisticated European mainland as a lesser, emasculated world. Another Corsican named Napoleon Buonaparte had not too long before almost subjugated the entire continent to his will, and was only defeated by the determination of another tough island race that was soon to repeat its task, this time against Hitler.

Born in 1878, by the time he was 24 de Moro-Giafferi was the youngest ever member of the Paris bar. Political from a very early age, he was made a Deputy (Representative) for Corsica when he was just thirty-one, in 1919. In between qualifying as a lawyer and becoming an accredited politician, he had fought the Germans in the First World War, been wounded at Verdun, decorated, and promoted lieutenant.[17] Vincent de Moro-Giafferi was not a man to take things easy, and was obviously one to have on your side. He was large and imposing, with a jolly face that could darken quickly, like thunder-clouds in a summer sky. He bearishly carried his large stomach before him, was quick-tempered and forgivably egotistical. Above all he was a performer with unparalleled oratorical skills: mobs of lawyers crowded into courtrooms when de Moro-Giafferi was at work. He only ever lost one case, and that the defence of a gruesome mass-murderer who was bang-to-rights anyway. It was almost as if, superstitiously, de Moro-Giafferi thought he should lose *something*, lest he anger the gods – but still chose a case so outlandishly impossible to win that had he managed it, his immortality would have been instantly assured.

The celebrity status of Herschel's lawyer intensely annoyed the Nazis, as did of course his sheer skill and accomplishment. They also realised how directly dangerous de Moro Giafferi could be to the Nazi cause, and were wary about confronting him in open court. In 1933, for example, he had organised in Paris a mock trial which sought to expose the real criminals and arsonists behind the Reichstag fire. The Nazis had cashiered some petty crooks and communists, and executed one of them after a piece of sham justice. De Moro-Giafferi proved conclusively to the watching world that it was the Nazis themselves who, ineptly and foolishly, had burned down the government building in order to suspend the constitution and justify the draconian powers they wished to arrogate.[18]

To begin with, however, the Nazis were easy to deal with compared to the Grynszpans and their existing lawyers. Poor de Moro-Giafferi had inadvertently trodden on a hornet's nest. With uncle Abraham in prison, his brother Salomon was jostling with Chawa's brother for the position of head of family. This situation was resolved only after Abraham Berenbaum travelled to Poland to receive a formal endorsement from Sendel, Herschel's father. It is notable that Sendel preferred a brother-in-law once-removed to his own brother, and underlines the feeling that Salomon was an annoyance to all involved. Salomon was thus headed off at the pass, and a proper organisation began to be formed.

But there were yet other problems. In addition to Szwarc and Vésinne-Larue, another attorney, Maître Frankel, had been engaged. De Moro-Giafferi did not mind retaining that man, but he wanted to engage another, Maître Weill-Goudchaux, for three reasons. Firstly, the two men knew each other and got along well. Secondly, Weill-Goudchaux spoke Yiddish and so could 'hand-hold' Herschel, with whom de Moro-Giafferi had frankly not much in common, as we shall see. Thirdly he was a more senior lawyer than the others, and could be trusted to carry out secondary duties competently. But Szwarc and Vésinne-Larue were, it must be said, quite summarily dismissed and felt their noses were put out of joint by it.[19] In fact they threatened de Moro-Giafferi with a complaint to the Paris bar. After all, these men were being compelled to forego quite a good bit of publicity – not to mention, they hinted between the lines, a hefty fee. De Moro-Giafferi had no time for all this rubbish. Having looked at what he was up against, he had simply taken an executive decision: get rid of the dead weight. It was Nazi Germany, with all the power and resources it could bring to bear on the case, that he was up against, and not some shyster lawyer from out of town. Luckily, money from Dorothy Thompson's Journalists' Defence Fund had been wired through by now, and de Moro-Giafferi used a good chunk of it to dispense with the nuisance of Monsieurs Szwarc and Vésinne-Larue, paying each of them 22,000 francs ($2200), which served to shut them up.

As for his own fee, de Moro-Giafferi generously wrote to Dorothy Thompson saying that he would accept whatever the Fund could afford. He was practically the highest paid lawyer in France, and in the end, for a case that dragged on for nearly two years until the time the Nazis invaded France, he rewarded himself not one centime. Nevertheless, he took some flak from Dorothy Thompson after laying out the money to be rid of Herschel's original lawyers. Perhaps she thought he was helping himself. At any rate, he was soon forgiven, and Dorothy was writing enthusiastically how de Moro-Giafferi had responded to the poison pen letters that had been arriving from Germany at his office:

> Moro has received innumerable threatening letters since he promised to take the case. He is a Corsican, and has official-ly warned the German Embassy that, unfortunately, his people, not being as civilised as the Jews, believe in the blood feud, and that if anything happens to him he fears there will not be one person dead in the German Embassy but they will be lucky if there is one alive.[20]

So it was that, with family brushfires finally damped down, the united front of Herschel's defence was lined up, with de Moro-Giafferi ready to unleash his devious strategies against the scheming Nazis.

CHAPTER NINE

MANŒUVRES

The Nazis had taken good advantage both of the quarrelling within Herschel's family, and their knowledge that, as vom Rath was destined to die, there was bound to be a murder trial. Proof of this last was that as early as 8 November (while the unfortunate vom Rath still lived), Hitler sent an express order that none other than Freidrich Grimm, professor of international law at the University of Münster, and de Moro-Giafferi's extreme right-wing doppelgänger, should be appointed to look after German interests in the case. Goebbels was to arrange the appointment, and Wolfgang Diewerge, a propaganda minister, was to co-ordinate the Nazi prosecution arrangements to ensure maximum publicity. Diewerge had worked with Grimm before, defending various Nazi troublemakers and prosecuting the assassin of Gustloff in Switzerland. Both adored seeing their names in the newspapers and thought they made a great team. The trial of Herschel was to be their finest hour.[1]

Insinuating Grimm into the French legal process was not an entirely straightforward operation, though. For a start, as he was

German, Grimm had no credentials with the French bar and so could not speak in the courtroom. Also, it was not Nazi Germany that was the plaintiff but the vom Rath family. Two things were needed, then: the consent of Ernst vom Rath's father, and a French legal proxy who could be trusted to exercise the will of Grimm – and behind him the interests and desires of the Nazi Reich – during the trial of Herschel. The first condition was satisfied in mid-November, even before Ernst vom Rath had been buried.

At the hotel *Breitenbacher Hof*, in the vom Raths' home town of Düsseldorf foregathered the heavy guns of the Nazi legal artillery: Grimm, Foreign Ministry officials, one of Hitler's personal adjutants, Secretary of State von Weissacker, and the ubiquitous Diewerge. Vom Rath senior was summoned to give his agreement that Grimm should represent the interests of the family. Herr vom Rath took along his family for moral support and announced that he would prefer 'to bear his grief silently and in private'.[2] In other words he was not at all keen for the death of his son to be used by the Nazis for the making of political capital. Whether he was blackmailed or browbeaten is unknown, but by the end of the meeting at the hotel he had given his consent, and ceded all his rights in the case to Grimm. Except for one interview with the presiding magistrate, Tesnière, for which he travelled to Paris, Herr vom Rath had nothing more to do with the case. Thus it was that by the time of Ernst vom Rath's funeral, the legal infrastructure of the prosecution was up and running at the German end.

That left the problem of finding a trustworthy French lawyer to enunciate the Nazi argument in Paris. But Grimm helped out in this respect. He travelled directly from Düsseldorf to Paris after the funeral and saw M Charpentier, head of the Paris bar. From him, Grimm was given the nod to go and find a suitable attorney – and he knew exactly who to turn to: Maître Maurice Garçon. The two men had been friends since just after the First World War, when the Frenchman had won a case in the courts martial against the German. But the verdict was obviously fixed in a way that exonerated a clearly guilty Frenchman. Garçon had done his legal duty but was disgusted at how the German soldiers who had been found guilty and imprisoned had been treated by French justice. He sued for the release of the imprisoned Germans and was successful. Since then, Grimm and Garçon had remained firm friends. But Garçon was a principled man, as this anecdote makes clear. He only agreed to take on the Herschel case on two conditions. Firstly, that he be officially named as the prosecuting lawyer, so that the final say in any courtroom manœuvrings would be his alone. Secondly, that there would be no Nazi racist dogma attached to his prosecution.[3] This was agreeable to Grimm, who was happy to let the trial itself be conducted as a strictly criminal case, but was left free to propagandise against the Jews in all other places.

Grimm was to act as a conduit between proceedings in Paris and the propaganda masterminds in Germany. From the beginning he submitted detailed reports and strategic ideas to the Ministries of Foreign affairs and of Propaganda in Berlin. In return, he was primed as to the extent of his own tasks in respect of the Herschel case and the Nazis' wider ambitions. Chief amongst these was the imperative to ensure the trial did not function as a forum for international disclosure of what was actually going on in Germany. At all costs, the Nazis' indefensible anti-semitism was not to be generally broadcast by the defence. Thus, his job was really to lean on Judge Tesnière, and persuade him that it would be in the best Franco-German interests for the trial to concentrate simply on the fact of the assassination, and not at all on the politics behind it. He should not have worried, for the French government and Tesnière himself had already come around to that view. Both would prove extremely pliable in this respect.

After this came the job of amassing information detrimental to the defence as a whole and to the Grynszpans personally. A search for every Grynszpan living within the German Reich was begun, the purpose to establish the criminality of the whole clan. Needless to say they found almost nothing of use except an old pickpocket, who was actually unrelated to the Grynszpans but shared a similar name. This unfortunate individual quickly found himself the centre of attention for a whole battery of eugenic specialists and Gestapo interrogators. The Grynszpans themselves, despite Nazi searches going back years to the time that records began, emerged as being practically the most law-abiding family in Germany.[4]

Another thrust of Grimm's strategic preparations was to establish the undoubted existence of the vast network of conspirators which had helped to equip Herschel and arrange the assassination of vom Rath. This was ultimately a big disappointment as well, but in the meantime considerable resources were put at Grimm's disposal. He was also charged with concocting a workable fiction concerning the affair of the Polish-German Jews. First, he had to assemble an account of how intensely humane and comfortable were the actual expulsions that led indirectly to Herschel purchasing his revolver. Second, he had to fabricate a political situation between Germany and Poland that was the reason for the expulsion of the 'Poles' from Germany. Thus it would be because of an international tension that the 12,000 were forcibly repatriated, rather than the simple fact that they were Jewish. It was a comprehensive and devious set of aims, which if attained would have the effect of pulling the rug from under the Grynszpan defence. Of course the world would know it was false, but reality was kept at bay for both the Germans and the French by the need to minimise the potential conflict between the two countries. The plight of the Jews that Herschel had sought to bring to light would have to be sacrificed on the altar of political expediency.

But the Nazis (and French justice) still had the indefatigable de Moro-Giafferi to deal with. His aims were two-fold. As a ferocious anti-Nazi he naturally wanted to present them in the worst possible light in court. This was, needless to say, Herschel's only desire, to the point of obstinacy. But De Moro-Giafferi also wanted to get his young charge acquitted if at all possible, and he knew that this could not be done if Herschel attempted to make political speeches. Apart from anything else, the lawyer knew that the court was uninterested in Herschel's political motive for the crime, and that he was to be tried as a common murderer. De Moro-Giaferri had to come up with another way to discredit the Nazis and, at the same time, get Herschel released. It did not take him very long, as we shall see.

First, though, he had to defend uncle Abraham and aunt Chawa against the charges those two unfortunate people were up against, of illegally harbouring an alien. Luckily the Nazis were not particularly concerned with seeing them punished, even though there was an additional charge of conspiracy to murder. Tesnière asked Grimm how hard he should be on the couple, and Grimm, after checking with his ministerial boss Diewerge, replied that the Paris Grynszpans were of no moment. That meant an example was not to be made of them, and that they would only be punished to the extent of French law on the lesser charge.[5]

Abraham and Chawa were in a pathetic situation, as they helplessly made plain during their original interrogation:

> When Herschel came to our home he was in such a state of depression that it was pitiful. He was ill and suffering greatly from stomach trouble. Could we have thrown him out? It would have been inhuman. Moreover we had been given the legal and moral responsibility for the child.[6]

As a result of their family feeling and simple common humanity, both relatives now faced a year each in prison. Before their trial Chawa was imprisoned at La Petite Roquette, and Abraham at La Sante, where Herschel wrote to apologise and thank them:

> Thank you very much for all you have done for me. I will never forget it. I know I have brought you great trouble and misfortune by what I have done. I know that you are actually in danger because of me. But I hope that everything will work out well for you. I couldn't act in any other way. May God pardon me for what I have done. I did it because I could no

longer bear the suffering of our persecuted brothers in
Germany. I beg of you to pardon me, for otherwise I will not
be able to be at peace. I beg of you to let me know if you
should have any news of my dear parents and brother and sister. May God forgive me for what I have done.'[7]

Herschel was indeed sorry for what he had done – up to a point.
Nothing would unconvince him that his protest was wrong in itself,
although he was genuinely regretful that a man had had to die. In
fact he began to fast every Monday in penance for shooting vom
Rath. But Herschel was aware of the very public position he was now
in: his character already was undergoing subtle changes that would
enable him both to assume the mantle of Jewish hero and martyr,
and perhaps save his life into the bargain. The above letter for example, though heartfelt, is conscious of its role as a public document.
Cuenot is unappreciative of this fact, calling Herschel a 'solemn
fanatic,' arrogant and egotistical.[8] So he might have appeared, but
this was now political theatre, and it was amazingly mature and intelligent of the boy (the *boy*) to subordinate himself to his new position.
For example, it was unlikely that Abraham or Chawa would have had
news of Herschel's family before himself: the request was a
reminder to all readers why he had acted as he did. Another
instance of Herschel's growing toughness relates to the fact that,
although he desperately wanted to see his parents, he managed to
subdue his longing to the main purpose of his actions.

A British journalist, A R Pirie, had offered to bring the
Grynszpans from Poland to France in exchange for the exclusive
rights to Herschel's prison journals. Dorothy Thompson's
Journalists' Defence Fund for some reason actually sponsored Pirie
to the tune of 50,000 francs – which suggests it was being done over
Herschel's head. But not behind his back, for by the time Pirie
arrived in Zbaszyn, Herschel had already got a letter to his parents.
In it, he told them not to return to France with the journalist, as he
had decided he did not want the diary published. This consideration

overrode Herschel's earlier threat to go on hunger strike if his mother and father did not soon arrive in the French capital.[9]

Abraham and Chawa, in contrast to Herschel, were tried very soon after they were charged, on 29 November. The prosecution was not out for blood, although it wanted more than the minimum term of imprisonment, which would have been one month. The trial was in a small courtroom and well away from the main press circus. Few of the public attended, although a Nazi agent was there secretly to note down every word of the proceedings for Diewerge. The courtroom was, however, packed to the rafters with lawyers uninvolved in the case. The reason for this was simple: de Moro-Giafferi was to perform. If they were impressed, the Nazi agent was transfixed. He wrote,

> Moro started right out. His well-known tactic: To wear down the court, if need be, with his exceptional knowledge of the specific provisions of the law in order to unleash, at the appropriate moment – towards the end – his tremendous oratory. So it was now.[10]

De Moro-Giafferi went straight for the legal jugular, arguing at length that Abraham could not be tried since the law itself was at fault: it had failed to provide 'safe haven' for Herschel, a minor, as it was bound to do. The child (as de Moro-Giafferi deliberately referred to him) could return neither to Germany nor Poland. As for Chawa, she could not be found guilty of harbouring a fugitive, since to save herself she would either have had to leave home, thus deserting Abraham, or would have been forced to betray her husband.

In any normal circumstances this would have been a copper-bottomed defence: French law, not the Grynszpans, was at fault. But with the fugitive in question being an international *cause-celêbre*, things were not so simple. De Moro-Giafferi thundered on, to the cheers of the lawyers and the silent respect of the resident Nazi. The judge had obviously had words with the passionate Corsican before the trial began, to warn him off politics. So as de Moro-Giafferi spoke, sometimes inevitably being borne away on the wings of his eloquence, the judge would wink at him. This was to warn the lawyer off when the odour of a political point wafted in, and on the whole it worked.[11]

It was due to the international situation, then, that Abraham was sentenced to six months and Chawa three. As soon as the media forgot about them they were released, though, and this but a month after their conviction. More serious was the fact that they were technically ordered expelled from France. But that order was never carried out because Abraham and Chawa were Herschel's legal guardians, and he was incarcerated. When Abraham finally did leave France it was in a Nazi cattle-truck, bound for Auschwitz. He never returned. Chawa lasted out the war on a farm in the south of France, and later remarried. She even moved back to the flat on the rue des Petites Ecuries, but changed its name from 'Maison Albert' to 'Maison du Tailleurs' out of respect for her late husband.[12] In the end hers was just one of over six million similar tales of horror and grief.

While Abraham and Chawa were undergoing their ordeal, Herschel's defence had been in motion. Since his imprisonment the tide of opinion, not necessarily within his family circle, but certainly among his defence team and Jewish opinion as a whole (and Dorothy Thompson and those rallying around her), was to sacrifice the reputation of the young assassin in order to avoid further provoking the Nazis and so imperiling the German Jews even more. The family was eventually won around to this point of view, with reservations, by de Moro-Giafferi, whom we have seen could be most persuasive. But Herschel had decided his role was to be a martyr for his people, and a figurehead arousing world opinion; awakening it to the plight of his 'brothers'. In any case, there was no way the trial would not be political. It was clear that Grimm and Diewerge were out to slander the Jews both particularly and in general to help their case and their cause, so counter-measures had to be taken. To this end the World Jewish Congress set up an office in Paris to collect evidence against the Nazis. It moved into premises on l'Avenue de la Grande Armée and was up and running by 1 December. Grimm, meanwhile, already had two fully staffed and fatly funded Parisian headquarters in operation.

This, then, was one arm of the defence – not enough to satisfy Herschel, who only cared about exposing the crimes of Hitler's regime, but perhaps enough to deadlock the Nazis point for point in the courtroom. But de Moro-Giafferi, in true *Cosa Nostra* style, had been darkly meditating on the perfect way to fuck the Nazis up. The plan he formulated was still causing anguish and embarrassment for the family of vom Rath well into the 1960's, and has been the source of much gossip, speculation and rumour.

De Moro-Giafferi's reasoning – if it could be called that, rather than some primitive instinct for revenge and poetic retribution – was that of the canny peasant: one should always try to kill two birds with one stone, and two blows are always better than one, as your opponent is less likely to recover. This is especially true if the blows are unexpected. Well, they could not have come from a less expected angle than this. For Herschel to be acquitted without further ado, de Moro-Giafferi told his associates, it is necessary to say only the following: that the assassination of vom Rath was not random. Neither was it the cold-bloodedly planned and executed murder of a chosen representative of the Nazi régime. It was much simpler. It was a *crime passionnel.*

In French law there were concessionary sentences for murders committed in the course of lovers' quarrels. Immediately the charge was demoted to one of manslaughter, and often looked on with charity. This fact was a key component of the image of the 'romantic' French to the world at large, after all. But the real beauty of it was that Herschel would have no charge to answer, since at seventeen years of age he was a minor and therefore himself the injured party (vom Rath was twenty-nine). In addition, the international public image of the Nazis would be held up to ridicule. Far from being the master-race they would be revealed as the depraved corrupters of youth, and of Jewish youth at that. All their arguments and presentations against Herschel, and by implication against his race, would crumble on the instant. Even better, Grimm and Diewerge had been attempting to make out that Herschel was indeed a depraved character, citing the decadent nature of the area of Hanover from which he came as evidence of this, and presenting his youth club, *L'Aurore*, as a den of vice and low life. How well they and vom Rath would know! de Moro-Giafferi would have pleasure in telling the court.

It was a paralysing strategy and a claim which, even if the Nazis could disprove it, would succeed (the 'no smoke without fire' principle) in its objective of destroying the reputation of their elected martyr, Ernst vom Rath, and impugning the Nazi party itself. Even more, there was the rhetorical satisfaction of successfully deploying a masterful falsehood against a totalitarian monster that breathed lies for oxygen. Above all, though, its appeal to de Moro-Giafferi lay in its utter simplicity. It would of course need a supremely articulate and charismatic advocate to bring it off – but who other than de Moro-Giafferi could manage the thing better?

It was not a plan without pitfalls, though. As Cuenot points out, it would be an easy story to disbelieve. More importantly, it might encourage the jury to distrust the defence and suspect its 'rectitude'.[13] France was a post-revolutionary republic where every man was a 'Monsieur' with his own opinion, and French juries were notoriously unpredictable, especially where questions of Jewishness were concerned. France had not too long before given the world the Dreyfus affair, and with the current international tension, nothing positive could be assumed. But overwhelmingly it was worth the gamble. Herschel would likely as not walk free, or face a minimum term of imprisonment. Not only would politics be kept at a safe distance, but the safety of the German Jews might be enhanced: there would now be a note of hesitancy in the racist declarations of the Brownshirts; a few raspberries from the back of the beer-hall, perhaps.

All this was fine, except for the simple fact that Herschel frankly refused to co-operate. Either this was yet another example of his thoughtless egotism, or to the contrary evidence of his clearsightedness. We must remember that Herschel, uniquely and within himself, was on a war-footing: he had already declared war on Nazi Germany. Herschel had no illusions that by saving his neck, and the trial from becoming political, he would in any way help the Jews imprisoned in the Third Reich. He knew that they were doomed, and had no use for such trivialities as a plea of *crime passionnel.* Still there remained the philosophical divide separating the headstrong youth from the mature experts surrounding him. He had seen the future whereas they had not. He knew how he must act for the long-term; they were paddling about in the present.

In retrospect it could be strongly argued that Herschel's was the wiser path to follow, since the Nazis really had no intention of going easy on the Jews. Maybe Herschel was gifted at least with a profound insight into the true situation facing world Jewry. At this point, late in 1938, the full enormity of the holocaust soon to follow was still unimaginable, even to de Moro-Giafferi and the Jews themselves. Historical hindsight tends to be crystal clear, and it is only easy now to see how correct Herschel was in his wilfulness. At the time it seemed as if egocentricity (which was undeniably involved in his attitude) was the boy's sole and selfish drive.

Perhaps unsurprisingly, de Moro-Giafferi's meetings with Herschel were anything but a success. Like the lawyer, Herschel was passionate and impatient, quick to lose his temper (the more so under present pressures: if he did not shout he might well cry) and not given to compromise. Since only one of them could storm out of the cell, this part fell to de Moro-Giafferi. Afterwards he sent in Weill-Goudchaux to speak with his young client, who knew Herschel's culture and language. De Moro-Giafferi busied himself with preparing for the trial. The less he had to do with the boy the better. He had no love for Herschel himself. But the lawyer was mightily troubled by the advance of Nazi anti-semitism, and wished to use the trial to slow it down if he could.

There is a letter, sent to the brother of vom Rath in 1964, from a man who claimed to be an associate of de Moro-Giafferi's. The picture it gives of the tensions and considerations of the time is worth briefly looking at. The man, Erich Wollenburg, wrote,

> One day, and unless I am mistaken it was in the spring of 1939, I met de Moro-Giafferi on Boulevard St. Michel, and I asked him for news of Grunspahn [sic] for whom he was the defence lawyer. He had just come from visiting him in his cell and was revolted by the attitude of his client.
>
> 'That young man is a fool, infatuated with himself.' he said. 'He refuses to give a non-political character to his act by saying for example that he assassinated vom Rath because he had had money quarrels with him following homosexual relations. Yet, such an attitude in regard to the murder of vom Rath is necessary, in order to save the Jews of the Third Reich, whose lives are becoming more and more precarious in regard to their prosperity, their health, their future, etc. If only... he would deny the political motives of his crime and assert that he had only personal vengeance in mind, vengeance as a victim of homosexuality, the Nazis would lose their best pretext for exercising their reprisals against the German Jews who are victims of his fit of madness and now, of his obstinacy.'
>
> I asked him then if Grunspahn really had had relations with vom Rath. He replied, 'Absolutely not!' I said to him then, 'But as a defender of Grunspahn shouldn't you protect not only the interests of your client, but his honour as well?'
>
> It was at that moment that de Moro-Giafferi exclaimed, 'Honour! Honour! What is the honour of that absurd little Jew in the face of the criminal action of Hitler? What does the honour of Grunspahn weigh in the face of the destiny of hundreds of thousands of Jews?'[14]

The letter is an interesting document, not least because neither Judge Tesnière nor vom Rath's defence ever got wind of de Moro-Giafferi's cunning ploy. Given that the homosexual stratagem would have been kept top secret by the defence, in order to unleash it to maximum effect on an unsuspecting prosecution, it is strange that a man so shrewd as de Moro-Giafferi should be giving away the entire story to a mere acquaintance on the street. Wollenberg appears nowhere else in this tale, indeed is never mentioned in any document or conversation. The agit-prop he quotes sounds somewhat like the brusque man of the world de Moro-Giafferi was, yet if Wollenberg was so well-disposed towards the family of a Nazi, which is strange in itself as he was a communist exile from Hitler's Germany,[15] then why let the vom Raths endure twenty years of rumour and slander before coming forward? But let all that pass: the letter remains a good (too good) summation of the situation at the time. As for Herschel himself, he may have rejected de Moro-Giafferi's homosexual angle, but he did not forget it.

There is every indication that Herschel was undergoing a truly rapid transformation inside Fresnes prison, as the implications of his deed sank in, and he had time to ruminate on his utterly transformed world. The medical experts who examined him preparatory to the trial were unanimous in their opinion that he was an intelligent and alert young man, articulate and sensitive. This sounds like a glowing commendation, but was actually very bad news for de Moro-Giafferi, since the psychologists decided that, in view of all this, Herschel was completely responsible for his actions. There is an eighty-two page document that they composed which leaves this conclusion in no doubt.

Herschel's original story (one of many – he made them up as he went along, before he cooled and hardened) was that he had first dreamed of entering the gun shop, and later went there as if in a trance. The entire course of events on the morning of 8

November found him on a zombie-like automatic pilot. The doctors were having none of it. They said they had examined Herschel for signs of epilepsy and other disorders that might have led him to such a state, but could find nothing. Herschel also claimed to have been suicidal when he visited vom Rath, and that his intention was not to shoot a German but himself; that, or to empty his revolver into a portrait of Hitler. Either Herschel changed his mind at the last minute, or he was a fantastically bad shot. And the doctors again disbelieved him. Once more they decided that Herschel was quite in control of himself, and though depressed was in spite of his threats no candidate for suicide. But being impulsive, opinionated and headstrong, he was, on the other hand, quite capable of setting out specifically to purchase a revolver with an intent to use it as he had.

The medical opinion is fine as far as it goes, but it is also curiously limited. For example, there is absolutely no consideration of context – the fact that Herschel was on the run from several hostile governments, and was watching his family and his people being subjected to terrible ordeals. There is no simple acceptance of the fact that this was still a mere boy. There is no speculation on the possibility that, up until the point of his crime, Herschel had acted in a sane and mature way, attempting to resist the waves of depression and anguish that were flowing over him, and to deal practically with the difficulties of his narrow fugitive existence.

Cuenot himself is at worse fault than the doctors in this instance. In his discussion of the medical report, he unrelentingly seeks to depict Herschel as a vain, paranoid type (even where the doctors finally demur). He allows the most innocent and understandable of Herschel's statements, such as his avowal to his friend Nathan that he would 'never go back on my decision' to stand as evidence of 'rigid megalomania'. It is undeniable that the position in which he found himself disorientated Herschel for a time; perhaps it briefly gave him ideas above his station. He did write letters to many world leaders, but then he was on the front pages of the world's newspapers, and top journalists thousands of miles away were campaigning for him. He can perhaps be forgiven for not displaying an absolutely comatose modesty. Furthermore, he was pragmatically attempting to capitalise on his public profile to bring attention to his cause.

It is true he was naïve, for example in the way he wrote to Hitler saying that, if reparations were made to the Jews then he would forgive the führer for what he had done and allow him and the Nazis to make a fresh start. But his original lawyer, Maître Szwarc, helped him with that letter,[16] and as an inexperienced and distraught young man, it would have been nice if Herschel could have expected some sanity from his elders. In the end it boils down to the question of whether being paranoid means your enemies are not out to get you – and by that definition, Herschel was certainly not paranoid.

On the contrary. He may have been talking fifteen to the dozen, but behind it Herschel was learning coolness and circumspection. His twin decisions are indicative of this. The first, to insist his parents stay in Poland rather than let himself, through the publication of his diaries, become a public plaything and object of speculation, was a difficult but wise one to make. Many more experienced public figures could profit by his example. Already Herschel could see that his image was a large part of his capital: he wanted to retain that copyright, and in doing so not allow himself to be defined by others. He was discovering what real power was.

The second decision, not to pose as vom Rath's catamite, meant for Herschel giving up his only real chance of freedom. Herschel had astutely read the political situation and concluded that he was more use within prison than without. You can call that egotism or you can call it self-sacrifice. As for his character, his mule-stubbornness, it was perhaps the only real weapon he had. Cuenot says that eighteen years later at his trial in Jerusalem, Adolf Eichmann still remembered Herschel's aggressiveness.[17] Amazingly, he takes this as evidence of how bad an example Herschel set, rather than a picture of remarkable heroic resolve that could intimidate even a monster like Eichmann.

Later, when Herschel attempted to enlist in the French army to fight Hitler, 'to redeem the act which I committed with my blood and thus repair the troubles which I have caused the country which accorded me its hospitality [sic],'[18] Cuenot calls it vainglory – an uncharitable appraisal of the boy's intent, to say the least. And finally, Herschel remained a mere boy at this point. But what he had was the child's divine singularity of vision, miraculously arrested before it could mature into the jaded pragmatism he saw in the adults surrounding him. From now on he was a prisoner, and the harshness of his experience forced him to grow up fast. But he had a good heart and a single-mindedness to go with it. Herschel was destined to become somebody very special indeed.

CHAPTER TEN

PRELUDE TO WAR

One of the strange contradictions of the Nazi mind – an utter disregard for truth and objectivity combined with a passionately sincere belief in its own lying concoctions – found expression in the Grynszpan case. Time and time again the thrust of the Nazi investigations was thwarted by simple reality. For example, convinced that de Moro-Giafferi must be Jewish in order to be so sympathetic to the Jewish cause, the Nazis attempted, by looking into the lawyer's family background, to prove he came from semitic stock. This was a miserable failure (his family had been Catholics for centuries), but they contented themselves with allowing that he was completely 'in Jewish hands'.[1] The international search for criminals in the Grynszpan clan likewise turned up absolutely nothing except the wretched petty thief of no relation already mentioned; yet in spite of this, and oblivious to how foolish it made them appear, the Nazis continued with their hackneyed cries of racial criminality. Likewise, attempts to convince the French that the sportsclub *l'Aurore* was a center of international political terror and Zionist anarchy had utterly foundered. The French police had conducted an in-depth investigation and found that it was indeed an apolitical sportsclub and youth centre. The Paris Sûreté must have been ill-pleased with the Nazis over this.[2]

The largest component of this paranoid and delusory tendency was the obsession with proving that Herschel was the actor, the 'patsy' in a world-wide Jewish-Bolshevik conspiracy to destroy the Third Reich. At the behest of his government, but with perfect accord, Grimm had set up several expensive and wide-reaching enquiries devoted to rooting out the truth behind the assassination. What is clear is that these committees of investigation, though established primarily for propaganda purposes, were completely sincere in their endeavours. The more a mountainous lack of evidence built up, the more convinced the Nazis grew that this in itself was proof of a massive conspiracy. Regardless of whether vom Rath actually was an anti-Nazi agent, and regardless of whether Hitler or Himmler's SS knew this and decided for cynical reasons not to let Grimm *et al.* know about it, Grimm was encouraged effectively to delay the termination of the pre-trial investigation until past the mid-point of 1939 by taking up more and more time with new enquiries.

Cuenot reports that in the June of that year, Grimm visited Judge Tesnière formally to ask that Herschel's trial be put down on the calendar of the criminal courts in July. It was an absurd situation. Tesnière, somewhat embarrassed, had to reply that this was impossible due to the number of requests for further investigations made by Grimm himself. Grimm was even more embarrassed. He apologised to the examining magistrate and hinted that really it was his government making the request, and that he was aware of the contradiction.[3]

The fact that Grimm, who had no official relation to the case at all, was talking privately in chambers to the judge is revealing of how things actually stood. Gerald Schwab has collected some damning indictments of Tesnière's impartiality. He had no qualms, for example, about passing on letters to and from Herschel to the German legal team. Grimm himself noted that only those publicly available could be quoted from, but that the others were extremely useful.[4] When vom Rath's father arrived in Paris to be interviewed by Tesnière (his only appearance in connection with the case, and an occasion designed to scotch rumours of a falling out with the Nazis over his dead son), Tesnière illegally allowed Grimm into the room along with the prosecution and defence. It is a sign of how shady Grimm had been that the defence did not recognise him, and Tesnière of course said nothing. He did, however, dismiss the translator when he discovered he was Jewish, saying that vom Rath's French was good enough anyway. Grimm was ecstatic over his little coup, and made bounteous use of what was said during the meeting to stir up sympathy for the murdered vom Rath.

But the most revealing anecdote concerning Tesnière's leanings relates to his reaction when showed pictures of Zbaszyn, to where the German-Polish Jews had been exiled. De Moro-Giafferi had been assiduously collecting photographic evidence of the way the Nazis had been treating the Jews, and Grimm was understandably nervous. He did not cheer up when Tesnière looked at pictures of the stables the Jews were lodged in and remarked that the place looked fine, and that he wished he had had such comfortable messings when he was a soldier in the last war.[5] Similarly, Tesnière thought the photographs of the Grynszpans' hurriedly vacated apartment showed it to good effect as a pleasant lodging. Apparently Tesnière missed the irony of the snapshot which was, however, not lost on Grimm. He wished to rearrange the apartment so that half-finished meals were not left on the table: a jury would not look happily on such a scene regardless of the quality of the furnishings. But the Grynspans' possessions, he soon discovered, had already disappeared.

This information does not show Tesnière in a good light, and one can only repeat, in mitigation, that the Judge was under the whip of the Ministry of Justice, which had larger, international considerations to worry about, and that his attitude was partly reflecting current, nervous French opinion.

Despite the fashion in which the Nazis had been slowing down preparations for the trial they were nevertheless, given everything they had going for them, keen to get it underway. Earlier in the year Grimm had intended to capitalise on the political situation (the defence was unloved by judge, government and public opinion) by heading for the courtroom quickly.[6]

After 15 March and the Nazi invasion of Czechoslovakia, this changed completely. Germany was now an international pariah and the mood in France had swung about. Grimm was forced to change tactics and instigate the delays spoken of at the head of this chapter. The defence, on the other hand, now sought to expedite proceedings as fast as possible. The only thing the Nazis had going for them now was that it was still in the interests of the French government to delay the trial date: they still feared angering Hitler, and knew that with Herschel almost guaranteed to be acquitted under present circumstances, there could be big, invasion-sized trouble. Grimm's very role was now beginning to change. His reports sent back to Goebbels at the Ministry of Propaganda were mostly unconcerned with Herschel, and taken up with political developments in France.

Without de Moro-Giafferi lifting a finger, Grimm found himself fighting a rearguard action. The French government passed a new law in April 1939 banning racist propaganda (back to the drawing board for Grimm), and his source of plausible witnesses concerning the expulsion of the Hanover Jews dried up. All he was left with was the testimony of the Gestapo goons who organised the trains (and the bullwhips), and that would have left the Germans a laughing-stock.

Even worse, Grimm got wind of a plan to bring Herschel's parents to Paris in order to testify. This was perhaps the German jurist's ultimate nightmare, and he travelled to Warsaw to try to persuade Polish Foreign Minister Beck not to allow the Grynszpans to leave. Grimm's timing was not propitious, since Germany was already glowering at the Poles from over the border, and France and Britain had pledged to go to war if Germany invaded. The Poles replied laconically that they would do the best they could. In answer to Grimm's argument that the Jews would use the trial to propagandise against Poland, Beck merely replied that in the eyes of the world his country was already perceived as anti-semitic (which indeed it was), so he really couldn't care less.[7] Grimm returned to Germany profoundly out of sorts.

To add insult to injury, even Tesnière – once again a representative Frenchman, so to speak – had begun to change his attitude. His final report held to the opinion that Herschel was fully responsible for his actions, but he also delivered a bombshell for Grimm: Tesnière, recognising the Nazis as the enemy of France, no longer saw why the background to the shooting, namely what the Nazis had done to Herschel's family, should be excluded from disclosure in court. The only crumb of comfort for Grimm was that the French Ministry of Justice, mindful of international tension, officially declared that the trial would not take place until 1940. By then, things might have calmed down. Then again, they might not.

During all this time Herschel had been cooling his heels in Fresnes, finding the passing of time tedious and his position frustrating. He was firing off letters to various official bodies pleading for a trial date, but to no avail. He had also been writing constantly to de Moro-Giafferi, beseeching him to do something. But this was hopeless. The lawyer was not up against the whims of a mere magistrate but the highest echelons of the French government, which had effectively issued a veto on the trial until an unspecified future date. As a final effort de Moro Giafferi wrote to Frette-Damicourt, the public prosecutor who had appointed Tesnière, and he spoke in the strongest terms:

> I have repeatedly had the opportunity to express to you the wish that the case of Grynszpan come to Trial ... Today I can no longer wait to express to you my opinion. This case must

come to trial. My client requests his judgement – or freedom.
There is no valid reason which empowers you to reject the
request which is in keeping with law and justice. I don't speak
of Grynszpan's decision. He plans to start a hunger strike. I
naturally don't agree with that; I have done everything to dis-
suade him from his plan. But he has such a strong character,
this seemingly weak child, I have lost hope that I can persuade
him to wait longer ...

If he can be tried, he should be tried. Is that impossible?
Then he should be freed.[8]

No answer, came the stern reply.

Herschel himself proved that he was learning the rules of this
grown-up game when he had his final interview with Tesnière on 26
July, 1939. Seeing that salvation lay in complexity, the youth began
to pile on new complications to his previous statements – each one
guaranteed to make things awkward for the French. Chiefly, he said
that his original interrogation was invalid because he had not said
what was reported. It was late at night, his French was poor, and
there had been no interpreter. Oh, *and* he had been beaten up by
the police. Herschel also claimed that the owner of the gunshop
loaded the gun, knowing full well the implications this might have
on the question of premeditation and intent-to-kill.[9] One can perhaps detect the hand of de Moro-Giafferi at work here, which
suggests that Herschel was growing smarter in another respect by lis-
tening to the master he had originally dismissed as unsympathetic.

From March until August 1939, Europe held its breath. Finally, on
1 September, the storm broke with the *blitzkrieg* over Poland. Two
days later France, Britain, New Zealand and Australia declared war
on the Third Reich, and in Paris Herschel's world underwent yet
another convulsion. The Second World War had begun.

The immediate effect was to remove the Germans from Paris.
Grimm was soon after appointed consul general in Switzerland – a

cushy job and clearly a reward for his hard work – and he decided that a replacement for Maurice Garçon, the vom Raths' attorney in Paris and now technically an enemy, should be appointed. Marcel Guinand, a Swiss and hence 'neutral', was chosen. He was less a lawyer and more a spy, ending up reporting French and British troop concentrations and movements to Berlin. But before that occupation took over his legal responsibilities he submitted detailed reports to the Nazi Ministry of Propaganda, and more importantly secured an assurance from the French Ministry of Justice that the case would not be used for propaganda purposes.[10] This is incredible to contemplate, considering the French knew full well that Guinand was a proxy not even really for the Vom Raths, but in actual fact for Goebbels and behind him, Hitler himself. Perhaps at the time the French still thought that if they were nice to the Nazis they would be left alone. Then again, perhaps it is not so incredible: that was the thinking of all Europe and the League of Nations throughout the 1930's.

The assurance delivered to the Nazis via Guinand had the effect of further placing Herschel and his trial on ice. Any hope of proceeding in law was even further slowed down by Judge Tesnière being drafted into the army. He was replaced by Maître Glorian, who had other things on his mind and saw Herschel only once, the day before Christmas Eve (clearing his desk before the vacation, perhaps), and then inconclusively. Even Weill-Goudchaux received the call-up and disappeared from Herschel's life. Apart from occasional visits from de Moro-Giafferi, Herschel was completely on his own, seemingly forgotten by everybody except his family and his warders. He remained in custody awaiting trial for twenty months: a record to shame French justice.[11] But then France was at war, and unhappy about it. Memories of 1914-18 were still painfully fresh, and doubtless the lingering hope that the Nazis might even now turn back undermined a due process that could still have spelt trouble. The French government was not about to risk all (as they might have seen it) for one young murderer the public had already forgotten.

The French were certainly not actively appeasing the Germans, though, and as 1940 came around and the 'Phony War' continued, the welcome that Guinand had found quickly evaporated. It is an interesting footnote that in January 1940, Grimm heard of an anti-German film which was in production in Paris.[12] It openly stated that the Gestapo had vom Rath finished off, and this supports our theory concerning the 'mercy dash' made by Hitler's personal physicians. Letters seized by the Nazis from de Moro-Giafferi's office when they entered Paris (searching for Herschel was astonishingly high on the Nazis' list of military priorities, as we shall discover) disclosed that the lawyer knew all this and more. Who can tell what he was planning to surprise the jury – and Grimm – with in court. We shall never know, because the trial never took place.

CHAPTER ELEVEN

PICARESQUE

The invasion began just before first light on 10 May 1940, with airstrikes against allied aircraft on the ground. The boldness of the German strategy which followed utterly wrong-footed the French and British forces. Von Bock moved his armies through Holland and into Belgium, as the Allies expected, and they deployed the best and the majority of their troops to meet him. Meanwhile, stealthily whispering along the narrow forest roads, and camouflaged from the air by the thick young foliage of summer trees, von Rundstedt's tanks made their way through the Ardennes, to the south. As this area was supposed to be unpassable by armour, there were almost no Allied forces awaiting the lead units that soon emerged on the French side. By 12 May, General Hoth's Panzers had reached the Meuse, and soon after, Erwin Rommel's 7th Panzer Division was facing the weakly guarded rear of the French forces.[1] The allies were exposed, and at the same time caught in a pincer movement. In less than six weeks, France had fallen to the Nazis.

Herschel was forced to spectate from within Fresnes as the opening gambits of the offensive were played out. But not for long.

German troops were rapidly approaching Paris, and the French government speedily upped sticks and debarked for Angers in early June. Probably on or around June 12, Herschel, along with the other internees of the French prison system, was evacuated southwards. His first stop was Orléans, but the safety of that town had been wildly overestimated by the authorities, and soon after the Germans were nearly at its gates. Along with about ninety other prisoners, Herschel was handed up into a truck and transported in convoy toward Bourges. This further distance put him very quickly over a hundred miles south of Paris, where the enemy had just arrived (and where Hitler, almost in ecstasy, was visiting the theatres and opera houses as a first priority with his court architect, Albert Speer). It was not far enough, though, for on the way the convoy was attacked. Schwab thinks that German artillery may have found the range of the trucks, and indeed the Nazi Foreign Ministry liaison team reported thus. [2] But on that day, 15 June, the front line was probably a little too far to the north to make this possible. More likely, reconnaissance fighters spotted the trucks and strafed them. Whatever happened, prisoners and guards leaped for their lives, and everybody went his own way.

Six of the prisoners arrived at Bourges on the evening of the 16th, claiming not to know Herschel (there was no reason why they should), and he too duly arrived next day.[3] This is more evidence it was fighters not guns that shot up the convoy, as the trucks must have been quite close to Bourges for the men to have walked there so quickly. What seems remarkable is that the convicts, instead of claiming their liberty, were so intent on once again becoming interned. But Cuenot, who as an army doctor in the Alsace Lorraine region was in the thick of the fighting, had a theory:

> During this extraordinary period, it was impossible to know exactly what made sense – the individual, or an idea that should be furthered, or any gesture that should be made. It was no longer a question of disobedience or negligence but of an immense disarray and confusion at all levels.[4]

He adds that some of the prisoners, who above everything feared capture by the Nazis, decided that it was best to be under French guard. Herschel and several others travelled with an NCO whose name has slipped the clasp of history but whose cowardice and garrulousness was to cause trouble for several people later on.[5] They were in Bourges by 17 June, but Herschel found the prison hardly secure enough for his liking. It had in fact been turned into a makeshift way-station, a scene of organised panic and quiet hysteria, where refugees were camping out, and parents were attempting to locate through the temporary *bureaux* their lost children.

The man who ran the law in Bourges, the Public Prosecutor (or District Attorney) was called Paul Ribeyre, and he was a good man. When he learned that Herschel had fetched up in his jurisdiction, he arranged with the chief of police to keep it a secret, and not to record the name of Grynszpan on the prison register. The fact that this was so simple an operation, unopposed by any official body, indicates not only the general alarm and confusion, but also the change in attitude towards Herschel on the part of the French. Suddenly he had become – for all below a certain level of government – something of a hero, or at the least a precious possession.

Ribeyre and the police chief, whose name was Taviani, agreed that it was wise to evacuate Herschel yet again. The Germans were advancing literally as fast as they could move. The rout was almost total, and Bourges was now only just behind the 'front line', such as it was. The only road open was south to Châteauroux, and as the steel helmets of the Germans were already visible on the horizon, that was where Ribeyre immediately despatched Herschel. Bourges was occupied on 19 June, less than twenty-four hours later, and that was when Paul Ribeyre's problems began.

As soon as the Germans entered Paris it was clear that apprehension of Herschel Grynszpan was one of the tasks uppermost in their minds. Grimm was making a triumphant re-entry to the city he had been forced to leave not so long before. This time he had no need of pretence or subterfuge; he could play the outright villain, a role made easier by the fact that he was accompanied by his own platoon of Gestapo intelligence specialists (the *Sicherheitsdienst*, or SD). This band was led by the archetypal SS specimen Dr Helmut Knochen, tall, blond and athletic, whose star was in the ascendent due to his success in kidnapping two British officers in Holland before the war even started.[6] Herschel had a serious character on his tail, and it is another sign of how badly the Nazis wanted the young Jew, of how large he loomed in their minds. The Gestapo moved into extremely comfortable quarters in *l'Hotel du Louvre* on the evening of 14 June, and next morning some of them arrived at the French police headquarters, demanding Herschel be handed over. The rest were busy sacking de Moro-Giafferi's now deserted office, where they found much to please them. The Gestapo was less amused by Herschel's disappearance, though, and set about honing their interrogatory skills on the Attorney General, Cavarroc. He told the true story of what had happened – of Herschel's evacuation along with the other prisoners due to be tried according to *French* law – but was not believed. He was held while thorough checks were made, and only afterwards was he freed.[7] Until that point a concentration camp beckoned him. Cavarroc was not the only innocent French jurist to be terrorised by the Gestapo, as we shall see.

Cavarroc's testimony led directly down the road to Bourges, where the Gestapo arrived at top speed, and started asking very direct questions. They naturally approached the chief warder of the prison first of all, but he claimed to know nothing – and he was telling the truth, since Ribeyre and Taviani had kept all knowledge of Herschel from him. This worsened Knochen's already bad mood. He had lost track of Herschel and had nobody to blame, except, as Cuenot points out, his own side. It had, after all, laid in fire to the convoy and disrupted the flow of Cavarroc's evidence. Next, they questioned the NCO who had brought Herschel and some other prisoners with him to Bourges. Why they went to this obscure man can only be answered by allowing that the loudmouthed soldier had been boasting to all and sundry about who he had escorted into town. Now, surrounded by stone-faced Gestapo officers, he trem-blingly told his story once more.

After this it was an easy leap of logic for the Nazis to nominate poor Ribeyre as the culprit of their woe. If they did not have Herschel in their clutches, as least they held the man to blame. Ribeyre was immediately placed under house arrest, with a vehicle blocking his garage so he could not drive away, and a German mil-itary policeman in his salon. This man drove the already frightened Ribeyre half mad by ransacking his record collection and then play-ing over and over a song called 'Tout va très bien, Mme la Marquise' – psychological warfare to be sure.[8]

After a period of several days Ribeyre's friend, Taviani, displayed a measure of ingenuity by convincing the Nazis to allow their pris-oner to visit the police headquarters. The pretext was that the worst prisoners had to be moved and that this required consultation with the public prosecutor. In this way the close surveillance of the Gestapo was temporarily evaded.[9] Taviani had his own horrors to relate, concerning the hard time he had received at the hands of the German police. But unlike the cowering and blabbermouthed NCO, Taviani had stoutly maintained his complete ignorance of everything except the order to transfer all new prisoners to Châteauroux. He told Ribeyre to stick to the same story. That evening Ribeyre was collected from his home and taken to the German police to answer questions – presumably about his meeting with Taviani earlier in the day. Seemingly satisfied, the Germans let him return home, and the matter appeared done with.[10]

But the Gestapo remained dissatisfied. They were no nearer to finding Herschel, and after the Nazi fashion demanded a scapegoat. Four days later, on the morning of 28 June, they arrested Ribeyre at his home and conducted him straight to prison. Here a curious thing happened: Ribeyre, who was by now truly spooked, refused to enter the cell he was directed to at Bourges prison, and insisted on remaining in the office of the chief warder. The French authorities had been alerted, and very soon protests and requests for the release of the unfortunate public prosecutor were being made by Taviani, Albert Colombini (a local judge), a senator and an archbishop. At eight o'clock that evening Ribeyre was granted his liberty, by means of a release order scribbled in pencil on a scrap of paper. He returned home to find his friends and supporters foregathered, anxious but ready to celebrate.

Herschel in the meantime had arrived safely in Châteauroux. But as it, too, lay directly in the path of the German advance, he had to keep moving. Remarkably, it was at this point that Herschel's captors turned him loose. Certainly the military situation was daily growing worse, and spare manpower was at a premium, so perhaps a warder could no longer be spared to escort the young prisoner ever onward. Whatever the reason, Herschel was set on the Limoges road and told to report at the prison at Toulouse, about 200 miles plumb south. The hidden message in this instruction clearly was to get lost, but Herschel took the order literally. He set out and amazingly arrived at the gates of the gaol in Toulouse a fortnight later. Cuenot takes the oppurtunity at this point to speculate once again on the defects in Herschel's character. This time he showed proof of his 'inability to adapt to events and to figure out for himself logical and reasonable solutions for his safety.'[11] This , though, is an absurd charge to make. For a start, Herschel was very much a stranger in a strange land. He still spoke quite poor French, and his voice immediately gave him away as a German – the hated enemy. He was without food, money or friends. The Nazis, he well knew, were directly after his hide, and he had seen how they would brook no obstacle in their mission to capture him. Herschel had no papers and therefore risked terrible trouble from every official he met. The whole of France was on the move south and complete chaos and despair lay only ever a moment away. At the end of the queue in this wretched column of humanity, it is surely testimony to Herschel's instinct for survival and his toughness that he managed to last even two weeks, not to mention covering an amazing distance (nearly twenty miles a day) on what must have been for most of the time an empty stomach.

Cuenot thinks Herschel should have fled in the extremely brief window of opportunity following the armistice on 25 June to a foreign country (which one, exactly, he does not say), hid himself (again he does not say where, or for how long), or sought help with other Jews (of whom he knew precisely none, and who were all in panic-stricken flight themselves, but still soon to end up in concentration camps). Not for a moment does Cuenot credit Herschel with the intelligence that he knew these avenues were either already closed to him or just plain absurd. Neither does Cuenot contemplate the fact that Herschel knew himself to be of most value as a prisoner, and was also calculating that the security of a French – even Vichy French – prison left him his best hope for survival. Cuenot even argues that Herschel should have joined the exodus of French Jews to the southern- and westernmost pocket of France where a number found relative safety. That, after all, was where uncle Abraham and aunt Chawa were headed. Yet the Jews that made it there were still in the jurisdiction of the Vichy government, and thus at the mercy of the Nazis when all was said and done. As we know, Abraham was plucked from there and carted to Auschwitz, and did not survive. Also, the Vichy government knew of developments in the Gestapo's hunt for Herschel, and was keen to hand him over (though he could not have known this for certain). There would have been no safety anywhere, in truth, and by delivering himself up to the prison in Toulouse, Herschel was only playing the least worst card in a hand that held nothing of any value. The most stupid and naïve thing Herschel could accurately have been accused of was a lingering faith in legal process. By now he should have been disabused of all his illusions anyway.

One of the most poignant facts about Herschel's doomed odyssey is how near he came to finding those closest to him, even if it would have been for one brief last time. In the migration south, uncle

Abraham, aunt Chawa, uncle Abraham Berenbaum, and one of Herschel's lawyers, Maître Frankel, had all arrived in Toulouse shortly before Herschel himself. Even de Moro-Giafferi was lodged in close-by Aiguilon.[12]

When Herschel arrived at Toulouse prison and presented himself to the chief warder, he was told there was no room that night, and that he should find himself a room in town and come back in the morning. This was yet another hint that he should make himself scarce: by now the policy of the French was to allow prisoners a chance at escape, which if not taken meant that they would be handed over to the Germans if requested.[13] It is unknown whether Herschel, ignorant after two weeks on the road, was informed of this.

Penniless Herschel probably slept in a doorway that night; he might even have been stepped over by his aunt and uncle on their way home from a café. Whatever happened, they never met, which is not surprising in a town groaning with the lost and dispossessed. After this missed opportunity, Herschel never saw any of his family again.

When Knochen's Gestapo squad had arrived in Paris and gone directly to the Prefecture of Police, they had been seeking not only Herschel's person, but almost as urgently his dossier, which contained all manner of evidence and depositions. To their chagrin they found, as we have seen, that Herschel had disappeared. In addition, as Attorney General Cavarroc explained, the dossier was also gone. It had been entrusted to a man called Menegaud, secretary general of the court. As the government hauled out to Angers, he had followed in his car with some of the essentials of government, namely the State Seals. These had gone astray as Paris was in the process of being occupied. A judge who had remained behind had gone along to Justice Ministry only to find it abandoned. Lying scattered on a table in the Chancery were the Seals. He took them and handed them over to Cavarroc, who passed them to Menegaud. Without the stamp of the State Seals, no government declaration was legally valid. Thus in Menegaud's valise, stowed on the back seat of his trusty Renault, was the most important cog in the legal and governmental machinery of France. The other item in Menegaud's valise was Herschel's dossier.

Menegaud had driven as far as Orléans, where he had stopped for lunch. He left his vehicle, taking the valise with him, of course, and when he returned he discovered it had taken a direct hit from a German shell. The valise was too heavy to carry any distance, and Meneagaud really wanted to get to Angers. The sight of his wrecked automobile had unnerved the man. He lugged his burden over to the law courts, but like the Ministry in Paris, they too were practically deserted. The only occupant was the concierge in his small apartment. Menegaud duly handed the man his valise, and without telling him what it contained, charged the baffled janitor with taking care of it. The man gave a Gallic shrug and pushed the case under his bed. Menegaud then went on his way.

After several weeks of making no progress in finding either Herschel or his documentation, the Gestapo were in a truly ugly mood. In fact they had just recently grabbed Cavarroc again and were once more interrogating him. It must be admitted that the story he told them sounded an unlikely one. Just as the Gestapo's intimidation was on the point of turning from verbal to physical, Menegaud walked through the door, and confirmed all that his superior had been saying. He was able to tell Knochen where the valise was, and a civilised atmosphere instantly descended. That left finding Herschel, and Knochen had one of his best men, Bümelburg, on the case.[14]

Paul Ribeyre had bid his friends good night and slept soundly. The next morning, 29 June, he felt relaxed for the first time in several days. He was just sitting down to supper with his wife and family in the evening when a rap on his front door interrupted him. When he opened it he was confronted by three German soldiers who laid hands on him and carried poor Ribeyre away. This time he was thrown into a cell without any opportunity to resist. The situation was now more serious than before, and everybody knew it. A Bourges lawyer, Labatut, climbed into Ribeyre's automobile and daringly drove right through the German lines. Eventually he arrived in Vichy and told the Minister of Justice, Fremicourt, what was going on. A message was able to be transmitted to the Armistice Commission in Wiesbaden, outlining the situation. Whether that body would have had any power to put a brake on what the Gestapo were up to is not clear.

The next morning Ribeyre was taken north to Orléans. There he was interrogated before continuing on with his guards to Paris. He arrived at four in the afternoon and was kept waiting outside the Navy Office in the sweltering sun. At eight in the evening he was thrown into another cell at the prison of Cherche Midi. It made his brief internment in the Bourges gaol look like a summer-camp. Cuenot described Ribeyre's new surroundings as follows:

> This was a veritable dungeon, with no light, two boards serving as a bed, one blanket and bed bugs in profusion. In this prison were 120 to 150 prisoners of motley origin rounded up by the Germans from the lowest depths of Paris. A German petty officer, who was in a continual state of fury, ruled this abject, hunger-ridden realm of filth and terror. The officer sported a large revolver and high boots and discoursed at length, using the word 'death' as his frequent refrain. An interpreter at his side translated his harangues in the simplest terms, limiting himself mostly to the admonition that 'if you move, he'll bash your face in.'[15]

Ribeyre was kept in this god-awful sewer, quite literally in the dark, for eleven days. When he emerged blinking into the sunlight on 11 July, it was only to find yet more horrors awaiting him. The Gestapo had found themselves a plaything.

Ribeyre was taken to an interrogation chamber and saw just enough of the room to spot a handgun on the desktop before the Gestapo man barked an order at him. An interpreter told Ribeyre to stand facing the wall and answer the officer's questions with a simple yes or no. The session went on for an hour, and Cuenot says during that time Ribeyre found out it was the NCO's loose mouth had landed him in trouble; but in reality the public prosecutor must have been deaf and blind not to have figured it out much earlier. At the end of this terrifying interrogation, the officer flatly announced that Ribeyre was to be shot in the mid-afternoon. He was given permission to write to his family.[16]

It was at this point that all his nervousness left him, and Ribeyre found himself, as men facing certain death frequently do, in a blessed state of serenity. His mind was suddenly clear and calm, and he wrote an eloquent letter bidding his wife and children farewell. He also wrote a note exonerating Taviani and the chief warder at Bourges of any responsibility. The decision to evacuate Herschel, Ribeyre announced, had been purely his own. The most outrageous fact about the whole grisly episode was that when Ribeyre sent Herschel on his way it was perfectly within his power to do so. The Nazis had not yet taken Bourges and France had not yet fallen. He was not disobeying his new 'masters' and had done nothing illegal. Had it not been so horrifying, Ribeyre's incarceration could easily be seen for what it was: an impudent farce.

Ribeyre was thus left to make peace with his memories and his Maker in the stinking filthy cell. But he was not brought out to face the firing squad either that afternoon or the next day. On the morning of 13 July his cell door opened and two German soldiers told him to come with them and bring his hat – practically a code for 'say your prayers'. But instead of being led into the yard and blindfolded, Ribeyre was frogmarched back to the interrogation room. There stood Cavarroc, who flung his arms around the dazed Ribeyre. His ordeal was over. Indeed it had never truly begun, as the Nazis would never have shot him: not only would it have caused trouble with the

Armistice Commission, but it would have soured the atmosphere with the nascent Vichy administration. The cruellest thing was that the Nazis had known the whereabouts of Herschel since 5 July, well before Ribeyre had been interrogated at gunpoint and not long after he was flung into the lowest depths of Cherche-Midi.

Ribeyre, a gentle, considerate man, had been psychologically harrowed by his undeserved experience. He had lost thirteen pounds in weight during his time in the dark cell, and his nerves were unravelled. He was jumpy, starting at the slightest stimulation, insomniac and fragile. Cavarroc took him to be 'debriefed' by Frette-Damicourt, Ribeyre's Paris superior (the man who had appointed Tesnière to Herschel's case), and after attempting to cheer him, they gave Ribeyre an automobile so he could travel directly back to his family in Bourges. Shortly after he was offered a job in Algiers, and he took it without hesitation. So departed one of the best friends Herschel Grynszpan never had; a thoughtful man who took the law seriously and suffered for it under the tyranny of the Nazis.

Herschel, after a night sleeping rough in Toulouse, had managed to secure a cell for himself in the local gaol. There was no Ribeyre to look out for his interests here, and in any case no place else left to run. The Vichy authorities therefore were informed of the appearance of the lost prisoner, and after that Herschel became completely vulnerable to the whims of a collaborationist administration desperate to come to terms with its conqueror.

Knochen's bloodhound, Bümelburg, had been searching high and low without success for Herschel until he had the idea of requesting information from the Vichy government. This was before Vichy had broken off terms with Britain, but it was still worth a try for Bümelburg, who had exhausted all other possibilities. As it happened, his request (it was actually for Herschel's dossier), coincided with the arrival on official records of Herschel's detention in Toulouse.[17]

The Vichy authorities handed Herschel over on the demarcation line of occupied France on 18 July. Less than 48 hours later the youth was being interrogated at Gestapo headquarters – that infamous hell-hole – in Berlin. From now on Herschel was alone, at the mercy of his enemies.

CHAPTER TWELVE

IN THE THEATRE
OF HELL

At last Herschel was in the Nazis' grasp, and they had big plans for him. The grisly fate of his co-religionists was not to be shared by the young assassin of vom Rath; he would not be allowed to die in obscurity, but would be made useful to the Nazi cause. This meant a show-trial designed to reveal to the world the true nature of Jewish conspiracy against Germany, and thus justify the actions of the Nazi state. To his immeasurable surprise, Herschel found himself treated almost as a VIP.

The next instalment of this extraordinary saga is perhaps the strangest of all. A few broad brush-strokes serve to fill in the background of the new picture: a lone Jewish youth, now nineteen years of age, is a prisoner in the country of his birth, at the mercy of his racial enemies who are at that moment exterminating other Jews with an aim towards their extinction. Yet Herschel is safeguarded, paradoxically spared for the time being because unlike the innocents, he has committed a capital offence. In a way he had not intended nor could have predicted, Herschel's protest against the Nazis had brought him to a pass where his single impulsive action of two years ago now involved him personally with many of the most senior figures in Hitler's Reich. Entire government ministries were soon to be fighting each other for the privilege of handling his case, of merely drawing close to him. No longer a boy, Herschel was quick to discover that, contrary to appearances, he was not entirely power-less. If his first intention was to help his fellow Jews and cause trouble for the Nazis, then perhaps its execution, despite recent reversals, was still possible. For Herschel had inadvertently become the protagonist in an age-old drama.

The mental sickness of Nazism, emanating from Hitler as its source but transmitted and redoubled in astringency down through all lev-els of the Party hierarchy, was ill-prepared for the sheer reality of a Jew like Herschel. Perfidious as the Nazis' anti-semitism was, it cannot be doubted that such hatred was sincere. The name for it may have been paranoia, but it had passed into reality: the delusion had been trans-formed into the law. The Nazis, engaged by now in the Final Solution, were attempting to provide a happy ending to their own nightmare of Jewish infiltration, contamination and domination. Yet what remained, as Marx would have said, was an inherent ideological con-tradiction.

Ultimately to make their dream come true, and verify the story in which the Nazis believed (so central to their identity was this story that they could not have existed without it) was a tangible specimen of the Jewish plague whom they could hold up as justifying their enterprise. It was no real good pointing to the luckless victims lined up for slaugh-ter in the death-camps as examples of the *echt* nemesis of the German people. The innocent Jews were of the species, but they were not the Jewish devil himself. Truth be told, the Nazis were concerned that the harder they looked for the genius in the matrix, the further they were from finding it. Psychologically and politically, they needed to nail a Jew with some 'form'. Herschel, by virtue of his crime and the extra-ordinary sequence of events that followed, had assumed that mantle.

Here was a Jew who, according to the Nazis' beliefs, had struck at the heart of the German people. He was a young, good-looking, Dionysiac figure, a spry foreign sophist and enchanter, who had arrived to bring chaos within the walls of the polis. Herschel's elusiveness, so tantalising for them, had doubtless confirmed him in this role – a complex, deep and almost mythical one. The Nazis could at last touch his demonic insubstantiality; and touch him they did, but gently. It was not the pliers and branding iron for Herschel, nor the blade and the mailed fist. He had to be kept alive and in good health so that he could be brought ceremonially to the scaffold; he had to be fattened and oiled for ritual sacrifice, dressed in fine raiments and curiously honoured for the favour that he was to bestow on the Nazi cause. Herschel was destined to be nothing less than its ultimate legitimator.

To the insecure and obsessive Nazi mind, taking refuge in a sclerotic, sentimental ideal of culture, Herschel's credentials would be silently compelling. There was even the tantalising rumour of his androgyny to underline the danger he incarnated. And there was also the threat that he personified a forbidden desire, strong enough if denied to bring about the very chaos his death should end. And finally there was the fear that he would slip his bonds; that no prison could hold him. In one way or another, every single one of these outlandish possibilities prevailed.

As soon as Herschel arrived in Germany, he was taken to Gestapo Headquarters in Berlin and kept there. Usually nobody emerged alive, but Herschel did. He was interrogated but not tortured, and calmly reiterated his earliest version of events: that he had gone to the German embassy in Paris to make a spectacular protest by committing suicide before Hitler's portrait. Only the verbal provocation offered by vom Rath had made him deviate from his plan.[1] Herschel was unflappable in the face of SS intimidation, and his conduct even succeeded in intimidating his would-be tormentors. Herschel had the strength that came from knowing he was already as good as dead, and psychologically had passed to some other realm. It allowed his anger to simmer and his voice to remain steady. To the Nazis it only increased the impresssion that in a haunting way they were powerless before this strange boy. Their treatment of him softened; the questioning was civilised. On 23 July, 1940, three days after his original interrogation, Herschel wrote out his deposition in his own hand and slowly passed it to his captors. Then he sat back to watch what they might do next.

Herschel was sent to the concentration camp of Sachsenhausen, but was spared the deprivations endured by the other inmates. Instead he was confined in the VIP bunker, with other prisoners too important to be allowed to perish needlessly. Pastor Martin Niemoller, the courageous anti-Nazi churchman was a neighbour. Other prisoners who 'enjoyed' similar conditions at other camps later included Stalin's son, captured on the Eastern Front, and Italian royalty, Hitler's erstwhile house-guests. Herschel was surprised and almost embarrassed by his preferential treatment, which included freedom of movement within his enclosure, and rations identical to those his guards ate. He failed yet to understand his true significance to the Nazis. What eventually persuaded him was the absolutely remarkable attitude of his SS guards, as Schwab relates. Not only did they treat him well, nicknaming Herschel 'Bubi' or 'baby', but they treated other prisoners better when Herschel was around.[2]

Think for a moment on that detail, which Schwab lets drop *en passant* into his text: the SS guards treated the other prisoners, the despised Jews, much better when Herschel was there to observe them. That he himself was treated well can be construed logically, for it was more than their lives were worth for the guards to allow a prisoner to die when the führer himself had a concern in the matter.[3] Herschel's ease and good health was therefore a necessity. But the fact that his very presence conditioned the behaviour of the SS towards others of his kind suggests something more; it suggests a power and control Herschel exercised over his captors that is anything but logical. From whence it came has already been speculated upon, but that does not lessen its impressive strangeness.

What, then, was this power? Partly it must have derived from the disparity between Herschel's crime and his appearance, as the nickname suggests. Partly it must have been the further disparity between that appearance of extreme youthfulness and innocence, and the personality which lurked within. Cuenot tells us that between the ages of seventeen and nineteen, which he had spent entirely in custody, Herschel had grown in stature[4]: not having much else to do, and driven by his conviction and an inner rage, the boy had worked on his personality, upon his very self. He was now, despite his diminutive size, an impressive figure, and had gained a measure of what is recognised as charisma. Added to this is the fact that he was a scapegoat, an elected outsider, and such people by virtue of their selection (why this one and not that?) are automatically imbued with a certain supernatural substance. Whether it is good or evil depends on one's standpoint. That by his crime he effectively chose himself, unlike other Jews who were simply selected wholesale, lent him stature; made him aggressive in his apartness. In other words, the guards were somewhat in awe of him, despite themselves.

To this can be added the undertones of sexuality. As mentioned above, Herschel was a living embodiment of the Jewish menace to the Nazis, again something super-real and supernatural. At last the figure of their fantasies was before them. Such an experience may well have been tantalising for a dedicated Nazi, even amounting to a quasi-sexual thrill, and not necessarily a pleasurable one. It is no secret that the rigid sense of order, the erotisation of power, and the obsessiveness with hygiene (bodily and social) within the Nazi order is partly indicative of fiercely repressed sexuality. Conversely, the adoption of Nazi and Nazi-like accoutrements has for many years been a major form of expression for those who believe their sexuality to be 'deviant'.[5] This did not begin after the Second World War but well before it, with the special nature of Eric Röhm's SA and with

Hitler's own private loathings.[6] For an SS guard to be confronted by the living figure of Herschel Grynszpan, with his 'uncompromising intractibility'[7] and disdain for all the Nazis' trappings of power, it must have been a frustrating, almost humbling experience: as if this boy saw into one's own innermost, unadmitted secrets and shame.

One should not overstate this, of course. On the day-to-day level the façade of formality and procedure would not have been shaken. But underneath, conditioning the deeper relation of prisoner and captor, there may well have been something of the 'all-seeing' about Herschel, at least to his guards. Herschel himself merely despised the Nazis and let them know it.[8] Paradoxically, though, this only added to his power over them. Though nonplussed by the situation, Herschel used his curious influence to help other prisoners, while his guards remained somewhat in abeyance. It is an astonishing tableau to envisage, deep in the bowels of Sachsenhausen. But it was so.

Hitler had planned three showtrials, of which Herschel's was to be the last and the decisive one. But with such trials there was a built-in fault that relentlessly caused the opposite of the intended effect. Instead of justifying and glorifying the Nazi cause, the legal manœuvrings more often than not appeared fixed and unfair. The earlier example of this, as already mentioned, was the trial following the Reichstag fire, when the Nazis attempted to frame a handful of criminals and communists for the arson. The defence ran rings around the prosecution and made a laughing-stock of Hitler. It was made plain to the world that the Nazis set the blaze themselves, and the fact that brutal sentences were still imposed on the hapless and innocent defendants only served to disgrace the Nazi régime in the eyes of the world. This was not to happen again.

The first trial, however, did not go well. Hitler had installed a puppet leader, Eliass, in the newly annexed Bohemian-Moravian protectorate. Though a devoted Nazi, this man was an affront to

Hitler's vanity due to his popularity with the Czechs. When Eliass protested against the systematic ruination of Czechoslovakia by the Nazis[9], Hitler decided that enough was enough. Eliass was tried and executed as a traitor, but this caused terrible unrest and trouble (including the death of SS pin-up Heydrich[10]) which Hitler could well have done without.

The second trial was not actually a Nazi production but a French one, over which Hitler hoped to exercise his influence. At Riom in the south-west of France the Vichy government was to try the leaders of its republic and its armies. The accusation was twofold: that the politicians' blunders had led France into conflict with Germany, and that the generals' ineptitude had thereafter caused the defeat of the country. Hitler aimed to ensure, through exercising pressure on Vichy, that the world at large saw how Germany was provoked into invading France, and that the Third Reich was in reality a peace-loving and benign régime. But the French people hated the German occupiers, and the government at Vichy took cognizance of this fact. What is more, it was naturally disinclined to accuse its own people in the interests of the Nazis, and therefore dragged its feet. On the eve of the trial in January 1942 the president of the French supreme court resigned in disgust at the task before him – and the French heartily approved his gesture. The trial was delayed until mid-February. Though Vichy could not outrightly stare down the Nazis, yet it could more subtly resist. Political re-appointments and bureaucratic obstruction from the French convinced Hitler that he could not hope for the results he wanted from the Riom trial, and when the trial was suspended for the second time, after 4 April 1942, Hitler did not attempt to persuade the French to reschedule it. And they never did.[11]

All of this meant that the trial planned for Herschel assumed even greater importance, and in the light of the many previous mismanagements and cock-ups, its preparations were to be carried out with the utmost scrupulousness. There were only two potential impediments: Herschel, and the Nazis themselves.

If the Nazis had only acted as Nazis should (and usually did),
then Herschel could have quickly been tried and sentenced – his
guilt after all was clear, and to prove it was a technicality. But several factors prevented this. First and most obviously, there was the
desire for a show-trial to impress the world, which Goebbels especially was looking forward to stage-managing. It was almost
pointless to condemn Herschel without doing it in the spotlight of
publicity, but this meant that a copper-bottomed indictment and
prosecution had to be prepared. Harsh experience had shown what
might otherwise happen, despite the apparent helplessness of the
defendant. Secondly, there was the intangible but compelling feeling that Herschel was too special, too unique simply to dispose of
in the back alley, so to speak. He was psychologically valuable to the
Nazis, and his trial was a species of public exorcism. Thus Herschel's
condemnation should be accompanied by the howling execrations
of the mob. Third and most interesting was the Nazis', and more
specifically the Ministry of Justice's, interest in making all appear
proper and procedural, according to the letter of the law. This last
Goebbels could not give a damn about, but Hitler did (always he was
concerned with the minor proprieties, if not the major ones), and
insisted the paperwork and form of words be just so.

From the beginning of the trial preparations there existed a tension between State Secretary Freisler (and later Schlegelburger) at the
Ministry of Justice, and Goebbels and Diewerge at the Ministry of
Propaganda. This was further complicated by Ribbentrop and Grimm
at the Foreign Ministry (Grimm was now consul-general in Paris).
Ribbentrop desperately wanted to exonerate himself for his failures
and incompetence in France. For him the trial offered a very personal
form of salvation. He was convinced that he could get Georges
Bonnet, who had been the French Foreign Minister, to testify as a star
witness. Goebbels wanted nothing less than to place world Jewry in the
dock, for the very practical reason that the Final Solution required a
steadfast ideological underpinning. The Ministry of Justice, on the
whole jurists first and Nazis second, meanwhile disliked the way the

legal process was being hijacked by these various political factions. Declaring its interest in safeguarding the reputation of the Reich, it sought to reign in the more reckless ambitions of the politicians.

Beneath these three bodies lay the People's Court, which was to try Herschel, and which Goebbels sought to control for his own purposes. He did not trust the jurists, whom he felt to be politically naïve, and his suspicions were apparently confirmed when, in mid-1941, the Ministry of Justice instructed the People's Court to prepare Herschel's indictment.[12] When in the October of that year chief prosecutor Lautz finally handed down the indictment, it was without the knowledge of the Ministry of Propaganda, and what was contained in it would not have pleased either Goebbels or Diewerge.

In short, the jurists felt that the very idea of putting Herschel on trial was questionable in law. It was pointed out (for the führer's information), that Herschel, after all, was not German. Even supposing he had been, there remained the plain fact that the crime had been committed abroad and outside German jurisdiction. The argument that could have been worked up from the circumstances of the murder – that the embassy was technically German territory and therefore *within* the rule of German writ – was cancelled out by the fact that the embassy staff had willingly yielded Herschel to the French gendarmes. What extradition arrangements there were did not count in this instance, since they did not apply to political crimes. In addition, there had been no formal extradition of Herschel from France, so the Nazis' custodianship of the youth might itself be plain illegal (Herschel should be suing *them*). Finally, Herschel was under age when it all happened, and this complicated the charge of murder. The Ministry of Justice, to Hitler's chagrin, recommended that the whole thing be called off in order to save any possible embarrassment for the régime.[13]

What is perhaps most noteworthy for the modern reader is the concern the Nazis showed for legal niceties. They had, after all, illegally pillaged the whole of Europe, and were now starting on Asia and Africa. Yet a contradiction of the Nazi mind lay in its sense of self-righteousness amidst its criminality. Wherever possible, the Nazis liked to do things properly. It was just that they entirely lacked moral discrimination. To the Nazis, the bureaucratic correctness of a legal case, and the bureaucratic neatness of industrial-scale murder could both be entered on the positive side of the mental balance-sheet.

But Hitler had not become Ruler of the Western World by allowing such pettifogging details to stand in his way. The führer answered his pedantic legal servants by announcing that as vom Rath was a representative of the Reich, Herschel's crime was really directed at the entire government, and was therefore not murder but high treason.[14] One of the laws Hitler had passed after he seized power stated that 'The death sentence shall be given to any who undertake to modify by violence or by threat of violence the constitution of the Reich'[15]. Hitler, having survived the judgment of his own law, decided that it would fit Herschel perfectly. But the twin difficulties, of the *de facto* illegal extraditon and the wished for *political* trial (which would have infringed the French rules of extradition), remained a serious headache.

Diewerge acted swiftly to repair the damage done by this fragile document being sent naked as a babe into the world, bereft of its life-saving propagandistic swaddling. Along with Eichmann of the Gestapo, and Grimm, he drew up a new rubric for the prosecution that placed not Herschel himself but 'World Jewry' squarely in the dock. The Nazis were to stress the depth and longevity of semitic agitation in Germany; the violence that typified Jewish actions (list supplied); the machinations of Zionists that compelled the French to go to war with the Reich; the Nazi aim for world peace, which incidentally necessitated doing away with all Jews; and finally, for good measure, the all-round evil of the Jewish race.[16]

Hitler agreed in the winter of 1941 to let the trial go ahead (probably he had the rapidly developing catastrophe on the Russian front to distract him), and Goebbels gleefully announced early next year that the trial would begin on 18 February. It did not. Already there were many dark problems gathering on the horizon that cast shadows over Goebbels' energetic and ingenious preparations for a massive theatrical event. For example, the resignation of the chief of the French supreme court had forced the postponement of the Riom trial, the triumph of which Herschel's was to cap. The many French witnesses that were to be called were suddenly proving reluctant to accept expenses-paid trips to Germany. Judge Tesnière was in a prisoner-of-war camp, but preferred it to the freedom offered if he testified.[17] Georges Bonnet, who had volunteered a statement concerning the political circumstances prior to war, and Herschel's malign effect on Franco-German relations, refused point-blank to travel to Germany, though the Nazis threatened him with imprisonment.[18] M Carpe, the owner of the gunshop, could not be found. Some witnesses were ill. Somebody else's dog had died. The Nazis found this lack of co-operation inexplicable: they were simply unable to imagine that the fact that France had been invaded had to some extent turned the French against them.

On top of this the Ministry of Justice was beginning to enjoy itself. After Goebbels had gone to the immense trouble of booking the 250-seat main courtroom, organising the catering and scheduling a detailed press-conference programme with plenty of 'scoops' for foreign journalists, Schlegelburger sent a laconic memo informing the propaganda chief that before anything political happened, the approval of the Ministry of Justice was needed. As a result Goebbels sought to wrest control of the trial from the jurists, and he sought to place his own man, Otto Thierack (a nasty piece of work and the judge who had condemned Eliass) in charge of the People's Court for this trial. Soon, he had secured Hitler's verbal assurance that this was fine. But in Hitler's typically absent-minded and contradictory fashion, he neglected to put his order in writing, and did not mention the matter to Schlegelberger. As a result, the Ministry of Justice took great pleasure in acting as if nothing had changed.[19]

In the usual course of things, Goebbels would have had no hesitation in ignoring the attitude of the recalcitrant jurists. Had things been going smoothly, he could easily have weathered Thierack's protestations that nothing official had come from the führer concerning his new appointment. But a terrible new problem had arisen that belittled all the others. It had to do with the contents of the original indictment. Briefly, it contained a paragraph that made fleeting but unalterable references to certain accusations of a homosexual relationship between Herschel and vom Rath. To the reader this detail of the original case will come as no surprise, as it had been de Moro-Giafferi's intent to use the revelation as his secret weapon. But as it was a well-kept secret, Judge Tesnière had never got wind of the stratagem. As all the Nazis had to go on were the two bulging files they had 'liberated' from the French authorities after the invasion, which of course did not refer to it either, they had no idea that the word 'homosexual' had ever been uttered in relation to the Herschel Grynszpan case.

The jurists at the Ministry of Justice knew very well, though, because the psychiatrists they had commissioned to write fresh reports on Herschel had interviewed him in Sachsenhausen. Herschel, who had previously dismissed the homosexual ploy as beneath his dignity, resurrected it before the German psychiatrists, this time with bells and whistles attached. One of them, Dr Rommeney, recalled what Herschel had told him:

> Herschel gave us, as a reason for his crime, despair, an infinite despair, and a profound discouragement because vom Rath had deceived and tricked him. Ernst vom Rath, with whom he had for some time past had homosexual relations, had promised to arrange things so that his parents would not be deported to Poland.[20]

Cuenot himself gives fuller details of Herschel's story, which are worth quoting at length.

> Grynszpan recounted that one Saturday afternoon (he gives the exact day and date) he was loitering as usual at the Place de la Republique. A distinguished, and very striking-looking

gentleman, dressed in a light coloured overcoat approached
him and took him in a taxi to an assignation hotel in
Montmartre where for a fee he took advantage of him. A new
rendez-vous was agreed on for a few days later, but Grynszpan
did not go because it was so distasteful to him. Several days
later (he again gives the precise date) this person came to wait
for him outside his uncle's house on rue des Petites Ecuries
to try to get another rendez-vous. [Herschel] refused. He was
so revolted by his partner's conduct that, to terminate the
affair, he went to the Embassy on November 7 to demand retribution for the affront. At the Embassy, there was an
exchange of insults following which he took out his revolver
and shot his interlocutor.[21]

Whether money or favours (or both) were involved is unimportant. Herschel was obviously cunning enough to take advantage of
Teutonic pedantry and make sure he gave conflicting versions,
which would ensure some discussion among his interrogators found
its way onto an official document. Cuenot raves against this 'incredible story' because – guess what – it was clearly untrue, and a slander
against the highly moral vom Rath. He points out that Herschel did
not even know vom Rath at the date he gave; that vom Rath was away
(perhaps he was delivering transmitters!); that the German did not
own a light coloured raincoat; that Herschel did not ask for his victim at the embassy and that for days after the murder did not even
know vom Rath's name. But Cuenot again misses the point. In fact,
as Herschel grows more adept at causing the Nazis trouble, Cuenot's
already low opinion of the boy inexplicably sinks even further.
Amazingly, he takes Herschel to task for constructing this 'foolish
tale' and even asks why the concentration camp inmate made 'this
pointless avowal'.[22] Surely the answer is very simple. He wanted to
destroy the Nazis' case and make as big a fool out of Hitler as he
could.

It was this bolt from the blue that prompted Diewerge to move
the focus of the trial away from Herschel himself. By concentrating

on the Jews as a whole the Nazis hoped that they could avoid mention of the homosexual allegation. But in truth there was nothing they could do. As Herschel's homosexual story was in print, contained within the original indictment handed down by the People's Court, there was no way to prevent it being brought up in open court. A copy of the indictment had been diligently passed on to Herschel as required by law. Therefore the matter was sure to be raised. If the defence could be intimidated into silence, Herschel certainly could not: he knew he was living on borrowed time anyway. If it was mentioned, then the carefully organised ranks of foreign pressmen would have a field-day, and the magnificent show-trial would be forgotten, drowned out by the global gales of laughter directed towards the Third Reich.

It was just this sort of thing that made Goebbels chew up the carpet, and his immediate reaction, after ranting at the Ministry of Justice for being so stupid ('naïve' he called it) was to declare that the case be held in camera.[23] Soon enough, he realised this would equally destroy the aim of a show-trial.

Now Schlegelberger moved in for the kill. The Ministry of Justice still held a good hand to play against the all-powerful Goebbels because it knew very well that when the plans for the trial were submitted to Hitler for approval, they had contained not a single word about the homosexual dealings between a Jew and a Nazi. It was well-known that Hitler practically fainted with rage at the mere mention of deviant sexuality. If he thought that the trial was in danger of degenerating into a sensational sex-scandal, he would not have let it go ahead. All Goebbels' plans would have been ruined, so he had kept quiet about it.

On 10 April 1942, Schegelberger sent another laconic memo to the propaganda chief:

> Since the Führer has ordered continuation of the criminal proceedings against Grynszpan and the trial is to begin on May 11, 1942, I would appreciate early confirmation that

> the Führer, when he agreed to the trial before all the world,
> was aware that Grynszpan as part of his defence will allege
> homosexual relations with Counselor of Legation vom
> Rath.[24]

Goebbels, of course, could furnish no such confirmation. Other bad news coming in by this time concerned the redundancy of the witnesses who were to have testified to the marvellous treatment meted out by the SS to the exiled Polish Jews back in 1938. Those from the Red Cross would no longer have anything to do with the Nazis, and the representatives from the Jewish communities were now all in concentration camps, victims of the Final Solution the trial was supposed at once to play down and justify.[25] Goebbels thought he could survive those absences if only he could find a way to plug the leaking dam of sexual propriety. To this end he took the astonishing measure of confiscating the erotic epistles from the wives and girlfriends of French prisoners. These he doctored by the dozen to make them look as if they had been written to vom Rath.[26]

There was also the instance of some encrypted messages, supposedly written by Herschel using invisible ink, which were discovered hidden in the seams of his clothing. These messages conveniently announced that everything he had said about vom Rath was a lie, and that Herschel himself was the true and only culprit. And so on. Whether the writings were genuine is open to question. Where, for example, would Herschel have found invisible ink in a concentration camp? Is it not suspicious that the Nazis found just what they needed, just when they needed to? It is true that the writings sound like Herschel talked, but after observing him for two years, it would have been an easy matter to arrange some convincing literary ventriloquism. Curiously, it is Schwab who is credulous [S180] and Cuenot skeptical in this instance. It is perhaps best left to the reader to decide on the probable authenticity of the documents that held out a small hope for the (by now) pretty desperate Minister for Propaganda.

In his frustration, Goebbels had railed at the Ministry of Justice and the People's Court for their stupidity in handing over to Herschel a copy of the indictment which included the homosexual references. But the Ministry was not stupid; it was merely attempting to uphold some of the law in a tyrannical period. This was less out of human goodness than Teutonic thoroughness and extensive legal training, but it had its effect nonetheless. Goebbels forgot that Herschel had craftily supplied the Germans with the information in the first place, so it was not as if the indictment put ideas into the young man's head. On the contrary, Herschel was more cunning than that: he simply played the Nazis like a fish. He parcelled out tidbits of bait until his interrogators finally bit on the hook, and mentioned his outlandish story in their official report. After that, there was nothing that could stop Herschel repeating his tale in court and destroying the credibility of the prosecution. In short, his was a subtle master-stroke. Goebbels finally must have realised this when, after a time, he transferred his wrath from Schegelberger to Herschel himself:

> Once again it can be demonstrated with what perfidious infamy the Jews give one the slip when one wishes to seize them by the scruff of the neck.[27]

After this, there was nothing to do but admit to Hitler the delicate nature of certain allegations that might arise during the trial. Goebbels assured the führer that all precautions would be taken. Silence followed. Hitler was watching with horrified fascination as his Russian offensive fell apart beneath the onslaught of Stalin's Eastern armies. When he eventually replied to Goebbels, on 17 April 1942, he told his Minister for Propaganda to suspend the trial. Hope for a new date lingered on until mid-May, then petered out. Those involved breathed a sigh of relief: at least Herschel would not be able to make fools of them all.

But Hitler's real reasons for cancelling the grand show-trial must remain in the realm of speculation. The führer's confidence in Goebbels was almost always extremely high. If Goebbels said he could handle the sex scandal, then that may well have been good enough for Hitler. Cuenot thinks that the debacle of the trial in Riom had profoundly disillusioned the führer. After that failure, he would not even think about risking another.[28] That he was not more vocal early on can be put down to Hitler's penchant for letting his underlings quarrel with one another: it stopped them plotting against him in unison he believed, or so Speer says.

But most of all, perhaps, Hitler wanted to try and win a war that had suddenly turned from assured victory to the very real possibility of ashes and defeat. The Soviets were fighting back, and by late 1942 the Americans, led by Patton, had landed to assist the British in North Africa, and were punishing the German armies there. By distracting the best brains in the Third Reich, and therefore diverting some of the Nazis' resources for over two years, Herschel had done his bit for the war effort after all.

As a post-script a last word should be said about vom Rath, who obviously had no say over his posthumous legal dismemberment and the stories spread about him. The opinion of this author concerning what that man was like has already been made clear in earlier chapters. A tragic murder committed by Herschel against precisely the wrong man had by the end been redeemed somewhat, and perhaps to vom Rath's satisfaction, if he were looking down on proceedings from some heavenly vantage point. In the end, maybe he and Herschel were allies, and Herschel's victory vom Rath's, too.

There is absolutely no evidence that Herschel and vom Rath had ever met before 7 November 1938, and plenty of evidence to argue against both it, and the fact that they had been lovers. Herschel was lying not to save himself but to hinder the Nazis as best he could. Cuenot is incapable of appreciating this, but Schwab applauds it.

The question of vom Rath's sexual identity does not really concern us here, but it should be noted for the record that his brother, Gustav, a First Lieutenant in a Wehrmacht cavalry squadron, was court-martialed, stripped of his rank and sentenced to a year's imprisonment on 6 June 1941, for sexual offences with men.[29] Though this is a fact, it might be worth mentioning that recent clinical studies have shown that if one brother is homosexual, another from the same family is unlikely to be. It could perhaps be argued that this makes a measure of sense within the emotional dynamic of the family structure. But in this case it remains sheer speculation.

Schwab adds, while stressing quite correctly that vom Rath's sexual orientation is not really relevant, that a statement sworn out by Dr Sarella Pomeranz in 1963 (during a legal battle vom Rath's family fought against various libels and slanders) declares that vom Rath was in fact homosexual.[30] That Dr Pomeranz would know is due to the fact she treated him at the Institute of Radiology in Berlin for rectal gonorrhea. The doctor who referred vom Rath to her stated in his report on the patient that the disease had been contracted in the course of homosexual acts. Medically speaking, though, it is not at all necessary to be homosexual to pick up a germ so close to its heterosexual site of transmission. In other words the referring doctor may have been a prude. Dr Pomeranz remembers vom Rath because he was in the Nazi party. She, along with all the other doctors at the Institute, was Jewish. This fact even lends a little more credence to the argument for vom Rath being an anti-Nazi; for how many dyed-in-the-wool Hitlerites would have dropped their *lederhosen* for a Jew?

One last detail. Read and Fisher in their book, *Kristallnacht*, relate a piece of information that even the diligent Schwab has overlooked. The German Ministry of Justice in 1941 had discovered that Herschel, in Paris in 1938, had been vom Rath's whore and procurer. Apparently vom Rath had been known as 'The Ambassadress' and 'Notre Dame de Paris'.[31] Whether this was true, whether the French were having a laugh at the expense of the German Ministry of Justice, or whether Schlegelberger himself was trying to give Goebbels a heart attack will forever remain unknown.

CHAPTER THIRTEEN

LAST THINGS

Following the postponement of his trial by Hitler in May 1942, all formal traces of Herschel disappear. There is not one single further record or document in the Nazi annals that mentions this most difficult and troublesome prisoner. The implication is clear: as soon as he was no longer the centre-piece of Goebbels' projected show-trial, the order went out and Herschel received his bullet. We have seen that he was well enough liked by the Nazis who knew him for his end to have been mercifully quick.

Yet in keeping with the extraordinary tenor of this entire history, the reader should already suspect that things are not so simple. To begin with, if there is no offical testimony of Herschel's continued existence, neither is there a scrap of evidence that he died or was done away with. The Nazis' genocidal project was not, internally speaking, a bashful affair. One can perhaps swallow the tales told by German civilians that they had no knowledge of what was taking place in the woods at the edge of town; that the rising columns of smoke did not arouse their suspicions or anxiety. But the bureaucrats of the Final Solution noted everything down in the interests of neatness and efficiency. Given such macabre diligence, it is strange that the death of so unusual an inmate as Herschel did not warrant a mention anywhere.

There is also the fact that although the trial was called off, it was not cancelled but merely postponed. Hitler, in his trembling descent into fantasy, would increasingly admit of no defeat, no matter how trivial. A busy and pre-occupied dictator, he turned his back on Herschel's trial to concentrate on murdering his own troops on the Eastern Front. His earlier order, concerning the continued good treatment of Herschel, still stood. Had he found out about Herschel's demise, heads might easily have rolled. It is true that later in the war, from mid-1944 onwards, the more patriotic of his inner circle began to disobey the führer's increasingly self-destructive orders, but for two years after Herschel's 'disappearance', Hitler was obeyed in all things. This is a strong argument for his survival, at least until much later in the war. As we shall see, several witnesses attest to this hypothesis.

Both Cuenot and Schwab have attempted to gather what extant testimony concerning Herschel survived from the intense and chaotic period following the May 1945 armistice. It makes for very interesting reading. During the late 1940's and early '50's there was an interlude in the search for Herschel, which was reactivated by two things. The first was the attempt made by his father, Sendel, to sue the federal government of West Germany for compensation for the death of his son.[1] This action led, in the absence of any traces, to a formal notice of Herschel's extinction, and the issue of a death certificate dated the last day of the Second World War. As this was a legal technicality it cannot have any bearing on the real search. The second factor was an article by an old Nazi called Soltikow which was printed in a German magazine in 1952.[2] It claimed homosexual relations between Herschel and his victim, and vom Rath's youngest brother, Gunther, sued for slander. The case dragged on for an astonishing twelve years, with Soltikow finally absolved on a technicality. In the interim, though, public discussion of the entire case had been stimulated, many articles written, and statements given by various officials and fellow-prisoners who had had to do with Herschel in the early 1940's. An historian called Helmut Heiber wrote the first concise account of the Grynszpan story and published it as a pamphlet in 1957 under the title, 'Der Fall Grünspan'. It was during this time that Cuenot also began to collect data and compose his account of the affair.

The first rumours of Herschel's whereabouts started at around this time. A representative of the German Ministry of Foreign Affairs, Fritz Dahms, had been a colleague of Grimm and attended several meetings concerning the upcoming trial in 1942. He later wrote to Heiber, claiming that Herschel died just before the war ended. He couldn't say if it was due to natural causes or violence. Heiber, looking at all the documentation he had amassed, by contrast declared the following:

> While his relatives succeeded in reaching Palestine, Herschel Grynszpan lived in Paris under a false name, contrary to the regulations forbidding his residence there because of his crime.[3]

Heiber asserted that Herschel was liberated by US troops from the Gestapo prison at Magdeburg, and that they allowed him to leave. Herschel chose Paris, and was still there for all anybody knew.[4]

The judge seeking to settle the compensation claim lodged by Sendel Grynszpan asked Heiber to elaborate on the reason he felt free to make such an unfounded statement. Heiber replied that his information came from Interpol: the judge in the Soltikow versus vom Rath slander case had asked the police to look into the matter. Then, more interestingly, Heiber went on,

> Besides this, I would like to point out that Grynszpan had been seen during the last days of January 1945 in Brandenburg prison, where he had been registered under the

name of Otto Schneider, born on March 28, 1921 [Herschel's exact birthdate] and under the entry number of 3.520/44. I had confirmation of this from two different sources after the printing of my article. Walther Hammer, archivist and registrar of public records in Hamburg, wrote me that Grynszpan was under strict surveillance there and that he was transferred on January 20, 1945, to the local police headquarters in Magdeburg. However, I was told by another source that he was transferred to Hamburg.[5]

Already it is clear that Chinese whispers were developing. Yet at least Heiber's claim that Herschel ended up in Magdeburg in 1945 is cross referenced by having two unrelated accounts affirm it. Also, to believe that Herschel's arrival in Magdeburg somehow leads unproblematically to postwar Paris or Hamburg is wishful thinking. Sonnenburg prison (from where Herschel was supposedly taken to Brandenburg), was an SS collection point for political prisoners, and nearly 700 of them were massacred there by the Gestapo in late January 1945.[6] Walther Hammer thought that Herschel was moved from Sonnenburg to Brandenburg on the day of the executions, and then moved again two days later, on 30 January, to Magdeburg. If so, this would mean he was spared a bullet on that awful night.

Hammer's account is authoritative in tone and extremely detailed. After describing how Herschel was moved from Sonnenburg (it looks like he was classed as a common rather than political criminal, and that is probably what saved him in this instance), Hammer continues in similar vein:

> Schneider-Grynszpan arrived in chains at the prison of Brandenburg. After having passed through a dozen doors and portals, he ended up finally in a maximum security cell equipped with security locks and bolts and a triple door. He only stayed there until January 30, 1945 when he was put at the disposal of the central service of the Third Reich Security Police.

At that moment rumour had it that he was then taken to the police centre of Magdeburg, where he was executed by the Gestapo. But of this I have no certain proof ... The rumours that Grynszpan may have been liberated by the Americans at Magdeburg and might still be alive today seem more credible. It is even said that he went back to Paris and is living in France under a false name.[7]

Cuenot comments that for a prisoner, Hammer's knowledge was amazingly well-informed. This might have been precisely because Hammer was a prisoner there at the time (he had been sentenced to five years for treason), or Hammer might simply have been fibbing. In early 1962, Cuenot wrote him in an attempt to discover where Hammer came by his information. The letter the Frenchman received by way of reply is remarkable and worthy of inclusion here:

> Dear Doctor
> I regret that I must disappoint you. Since I am gravely ill, it is impossible for me to answer your questions. Moreover, I do not see any possibility of a useful exchange [of information] for you obviously have a fantastic conception of the events of that period of the so-called Third Reich under that ham-actor Hitler. We were so completely isolated that there was no possibility of my talking to the prisoners. I have no recollection of having made a deposition before the Hanover tribunal. Besides, after so long, I think that studying and explaining the Grynszpan case is a useless undertaking.
> With best wishes ...[8]

Hammer was dying and may have wanted to forget the whole period of the Nazi terror, but he certainly had written the deposition, which was in the Hanover court records. Was he lying earlier on? And if so was it to save somebody's face or to keep a dark secret? This is something else we shall never know for certain.

Besides the possibilities enumerated above, that Herschel was either murdered in 1942, survived until 1945 and was then murdered, or survived the war entirely and went to live elsewhere in Europe, there is the further chance that the boy's ill-health did for him at the age of twenty-one or -two, and that he simply died of natural causes in 1942 or 1943. The incentive to have kept Herschel's death from illness under wraps makes good sense: the guards would have been in extremely deep trouble with Hitler himself for so negligently carrying out their charge of looking after a special prisoner. Cuenot talked to Judge Tesnière in 1961, and was told this:

> One day in 1943, I received a visit in Paris from a German policeman who had received authorisation from the occupation authorities to examine my dossiers. I seized the opportunity and asked him a question. 'What's new with Grynszpan?' Apparently ill at ease, he answered evasively, 'I think he has met with a disaster.'[9]

This fails to make clear whether Herschel's health had failed or whether he was executed. The argument against ill-health comes from the descriptions of Herschel filling out and maturing impressively. His childhood nervous stomach had probably been purged by his ordeal. Frankly, Herschel just did not sound like a sick or weak young man after he had been in Germany for a while. On the contrary, all the evidence points to the fact that he was turning into a fierce Kafkaesque tiger. What is more, there is the absurdity of an ordinary German cop having knowledge of Herschel's 'disaster' and admitting it in faraway Paris. If the prisoner was dead, in contradiction of Hitler's order, then the fact would have been a fiercely guarded secret.[10]

The trails that led to Hamburg and Paris, though, were cold. Interpol's answer about Herschel's Hamburg residency was given in these terms in 1959:

> The information that [Herschel Grynszpan] might be liv-
> ing in Hamburg under a false name is based on
> unsubstantiated reports transmitted by an employee of the
> French Security police in Baden-Baden in April 1954. This
> information has never been confirmed.[11]

One of the witnesses at the Soltikow trial, an intelligence officer whose name is unknown, testified not only that Grynszpan still lived, but that he had seen and spoken to him in the courtroom the previous day. He claimed Herschel was prepared to take the witness stand if immunity from prosecution was guaranteed (amazingly, Herschel was *still* wanted for the vom Rath murder – if he was alive he would have remained a fugitive even after the war). The judge ruled that if Herschel turned up he would be arrested, so it is not surprising that nothing at all came from this witness's revelations.[12]

As for Paris, the plain fact was that Herschel's brother, Mordechai, had been living there in 1947-48. He was, of course, looking for Herschel, and made enquiries all over the city, explaining who he was. It was around this time that stories began to circulate concerning Herschel's incognito residence there, where he earned a living as a motor mechanic. This was in fact how Mordechai supported himself while he was in Paris. It was another Chinese whisper.

Surmounting all of these dead ends and uncertainties, there is the question of why, if Herschel survived, he did not contact the family to whom he was so close. None of his relatives ever received a single word from their lost son or brother or nephew. The only possible reply is that Herschel was indeed a changed man by the end of his experience. Schwab argues very convincingly that the disaster Herschel's crime unleashed against the German Jews had in the end a positive effect. Kristallnacht caused great suffering, and several hundred Jews died as a result of the thuggery unleashed on that terrible night. But the pogrom alerted the Jewish population to the real intentions of the Nazi régime – something that was too awesome and horrible to be contemplated previously – and led to massive emigrations of Jews.[13] That writer is certain that in the end, as a result of Herschel's action, more Jewish lives were saved than lost. And Gerald Schwab's was one of them.

But Herschel may not have known or felt this. He may have been crippled, if he survived the war, not only by the guilt of the survivor (which has been well-documented among former concentration camp inmates), but by his own specific and hellish self-accusations as well. It is not completely implausible that, if he lived, Herschel chose to punish himself by means of imposed isolation. If he was rescued by the Americans and lied about who he was, he could have taken on a new identity and started life afresh. Not to have contacted the people he most desperately loved could have been a sort of penance for his impulsive deed in Paris in 1938. One rumour has it that Herschel eventually lived in the mid-west of America, somewhere like Minneapolis or Cincinatti, and opened a record store. He might have married an American girl and fathered American children and never told them a thing about his other life. But if this was truly the case then how would we know? What this story has in its favour (as a super-possibility) is that Herschel in prison certainly demonstrated the willpower and resolve necessary to maintain such a break with his past.

It is at this point, though, that the current of rumour widens, river turning tidal. Even a random questioning of members of London's Jewish population revealed that it is common knowledge Herschel Grynszpan is currently enjoying a fine old age in Israel. It is possible that he has been confused with his father and brother, who moved there long ago. Then again, who is to say for sure?

What is certain is that in a sense Herschel proved impossible to kill. He has attained a further lease of life by reason of his obscure end. More importantly, by the bravery and cunning he displayed during his unfortunate young life, he proved that the hydra -headed monster of tyranny can be confronted and even routed. Herschel's was a small victory, but a significant one. His period of personal struggle with the Nazi totalitarians spanned the time from when the beast was ravenous to when it was badly wounded; from the time all Europe was threatened to when the tide of war had begun to turn against the Hitlerite criminals. Within that period, Herschel's aggressive resistance was a spiritual lifeline. If one believes that the invisible counts in human life, then Herschel's courage fortified the efforts of those who were seeking to confront the Nazi menace elsewhere. Simply by being there, proving single-handedly that the evil was not all-powerful, and could be subverted, Herschel Grynszpan strengthened and tempered the hopes of all the Nazis' enemies. In addition, Herschel's strategy had measurable consequences on the effectiveness of the Nazi régime, visibly robbing it of its last real chance to justify to the world its criminal ends.

Because of what he was, because of what he did, and because of what he became, Herschel is like a beacon in a dark night. He was not the only brave man; he was not the only hero. Many more still go unsung. But his life is testament to the spirit of the victim who refuses to cower before the bully. In a way, Herschel is immortal, his body fragmented and dissolved into eternal whispers of survival, from which we can all draw hope. We should wish on him God's peace. Also, we should allow him the last word,[14] which he spoke to a fellow inmate as he was taken from Sachsenhausen, bound for who-knows-where:

> Don't think that I am afraid. When I reach the end I will spit
> three times on this sinister band of rogues.

NOTES & REFERENCES

INTRODUCTION

1. Sir Michael Tippett, *A Child of Our Time* (Royal Liverpool Philharmonic Orchestra & Choir, conducted by Sir John Pritchard) & *A Weeping Babe* (The John Alldis Choir, conducted by Sir Colin Davis), The Decca Recording Company Ltd, BA 820 425 158-4.

2. Dr Alain Cuenot, *L'Affaire Grynszpan-Vom Rath*, trans. David Rome (1982) as *The Herschel Grynszpan Case* (Unpublished manuscript, Wiener Library, London), p. 76.

3. Klaus P Fischer, *Nazi Germany: A New History* (London: Constable, 1995), p. 436.

PROLOGUE

1. Cuenot, *The Herschel Grynszpan Case*, p. 34. This was part of the testimony delivered by Herschel's father, Sendel Grynszpan, at the trial of Adolf Eichmann in Jerusalem, 25 April 1961. Cuenot reports that Sendel was a vigorous old man, but that he grew extremely emotional while recounting his experiences, so that the president of the court had to ask him to speak more slowly.

2. Ibid., p. 70.

CHAPTER ONE

1. Cuenot, *The Herschel Grynszpan Case*, p. 8. The reasons for such terrible loss Cuenot attributes to four factors: poor nourishment, lack of hygiene, overpopulation and poverty.

2. Ibid., p. 9.

3. Anthony Read & David Fisher, *Kristallnacht* (London: Michael Joseph, 1989), p. 34. Read and Fisher report that in 1918 the chief criminal inspector in Hanover had 500 male prostitutes on police books (in other words, those were just the ones who had been prosecuted). He estimated that 40,000 homosexuals lived in the city, which meant nearly 10% of the male population was gay.

4. The novelist Thomas Mann's son, Klaus, made an interesting observation concerning the homosexual murderer, Haarmann. Klaus Mann recounted that in the early 'thirties he saw Adolf Hitler greedily wolfing down a succession of creamy cakes in the Carlton Tea Room in Munich. Something both attracted and repelled him as he watched the future führer doing to the cakes what he would later try with Europe (quoted in Fischer, *Nazi Germany: A New History*, p. 192):

> There was nothing but dim rosy light, soft music and heaps of cookies; and in the midst of this sugary idyll, a moustached little man with veiled eyes and a stubborn forehead, chatting with some colourless henchmen.
>
> ... While I called for the waitress to pay for my cup of coffee, I suddenly remembered who Herr Hitler resembled. It was that sex-murderer in Hanover, whose case had such huge headlines ... His name was Haarmann ... The likeness between him and Hitler was striking. The sightless eyes, the moustache, the brutal and nervous mouth, even the unspeakable vulgarity of the fleshy nose; it was, indeed, precisely the same physiognomy.

Fischer argues that the atmosphere of nihilism, depression and unrest in nineteen-twenties post-war Germany produced both Hitler and figures such as Haarmann (of whom there were a surprising number, and I would recommend Fischer's book wholeheartedly to the interested reader). He says there was a general brutalisation of the German population. Some of this showed up in perverted monsters and some in the great exfoliation of artistic and intellectual endeavour of the time. It was the period of expressionism – angular, disjointed and violent in its own way. (NB, Albert Speer also describes how, when finally he ceased to adore his führer, the obscenity of Hitler's fleshy nose became apparent to him.)

5. Cuenot, *The Herschel Grynszpan Case*, p. 8. Between July 1933 and October 1934, for the record, Sendel Grynszpan received 1028 Reichsmarks in unemployment benefit. After that, he managed to get back on his feet somewhat.

6. Gerald Schwab, *The Day the Holocaust Began* (New York: Praeger, 1990), p. 46.

7. Cuenot, *The Herschel Grynszpan Case*, p. 11. This was during the reign of Antiochus IV (175-164 BC).

8. Ibid., p. 10.

9. Ibid., p. 9.

CHAPTER TWO

1. Cuenot, *The Herschel Grynszpan Case*, p. 10. This is part of Herschel's deposition which was recorded in the French pre-trial medico-legal report.

2. Schwab, *The Day the Holocaust Began*, p. 58.

3. Cuenot, *The Herschel Grynszpan Case*, p. 11. Neither Schwab nor Cuenot actually name the people who described Herschel's apathy.

4. Schwab, *The Day the Holocaust Began*, p. 58.

5. Ibid., p. 46.

6. Cuenot, *The Herschel Grynszpan Case*, p. 10 op cit. Cuenot goes on to add that Herschel's teachers at Yeshiva could certainly not be suspected of partiality.

7. Fischer, *Nazi Germany: A New History*, p. 385. Fischer points out that it was The Reich Citizenship Law (*Reichsbürgergesetz*) which drew the distinction between full 'Aryan' citizens and mere subjects. Foreigners and Jews were of course subjects, *but so were German women*. This gives a little insight into the chauvinistic workings of the Nazi brain.

8. Cuenot, *The Herschel Grynszpan Case*, p. 12. Again, this was part of the evidence Herschel presented to the French medical experts.

9. Ibid., p. 13. The French immigration rules (at least for Jews at this time) were strict and absolute: funds sufficient to support the applicant for the length of his stay had to be brought with him. This effectively curtailed much permanent immigration.

10. Ibid., pp. 13 op cit., p. 24.

11. Ibid., p. 14. The Nazi ban on taking out more than ten Reichsmarks from Germany completed the Catch 22 situation (see note 9, above).

12. Ibid., p. 17.

13. Ibid., p. 15. Actually, Cuenot says it was *relatively* simple.

CHAPTER THREE

1. Cuenot, *The Herschel Grynszpan Case*, p. 67. This was the Soltikow trial. Soltikow was a tabloid journalist who published unsubstantiated allegations concerning vom Rath's sexuality (see also p. 193 of this book).

2. Schwab, *The Day the Holocaust Began*, p. 13.

3. Ibid., p. 14.

4. Cuenot, *The Herschel Grynszpan Case*, p. 65. As evidence of this, Cuenot cites the fact that in Munich for example, where Allied bombing had destroyed 65% of the city, the inhabitants greeted American troops with flowers. He rightly says that this may in large part have been relief at not being 'liberated' by the Russians.

5. Albert Speer, *Inside The Third Reich* (London: Orion, 1995), p. 47:

This was no ardent nationalism. Rather, for a few short hours the personal unhappiness caused by the breakdown of the economy was replaced by a frenzy that demanded victims. And Hitler and Goebbels threw them the victims. By lashing out at their opponents and villifying the Jews they gave expression and direction to fierce, primal passions.

6. Schwab, *The Day the Holocaust Began*, p. 15. Schwab says vom Rath was devoutly Christian, yet he did not attend church. I think it was more that his moral outlook was Christian.

7. Cuenot, *The Herschel Grynszpan Case*, p. 65. Mlle Ebeling also stated the following: 'Even though he never expressed any opinions about the Jews in my presence, I always had the impression that neither he nor his parents were anti-semitic.'

8. Schwab, *The Day the Holocaust Began*, p. 53.

9. Cuenot, *The Herschel Grynszpan Case*, p. 18.

10. Ibid. Cuenot estimates that there were around 50,000 foreign Jews living in Paris at this time, mostly clustered around Belleville in the 20th and rue de Rosiers in the 4th Arrondisement.

11. Ibid., p.22. Uncle Abraham also took *Pariser Haint*, the Yiddish language newspaper, and this Herschel would also have seen.

12. Ibid.

13. Ibid., p. 20.

14. Ibid., p.22 op cit. Apparently Herschel was not 'naturally lazy', at least where his religious studies were concerned.

15. Ibid., p.24.

16. Originally 1 April, but his father had managed to get it extended for two months.

17. Cuenot, *The Herschel Grynszpan Case*, p. 24 op cit.

18. Schwab, *The Day the Holocaust Began*, p. 60. Schwab quotes from a decree passed by the Polish Sejm (parliament) in March 1938.

19. Cuenot, *The Herschel Grynszpan Case*, p. 25.

20. Ibid., p. 20 op cit.
21. Ibid., p. 26.
22. Ibid.

CHAPTER FOUR

1. Cuenot says September.
2. Cuenot, *The Herschel Grynszpan Case*, p. 31.
3. Ibid.
4. Ibid., p. 43: 'Herschel must have been accustomed to the niggardliness of his uncle.' I can nowhere find the slightest justification for such an assumption.
5. Ibid., p. 45.
6. Ibid., p. 44.
7. Ibid. It must be said, though, that 500 francs was an incredible amount of money to be spending on clothes; and besides, the weather was unseasonably warm.
8. Ibid. Cuenot asks, 'To what decision could he have been referring if not to his plan for vengeance?' which, like his translator, I would query, though I would mention suicide rather than just a threat never to return
9. Ibid., p. 45 op cit.
10. Ibid., p. 46.
11. Ibid., p. 47.

CHAPTER FIVE

1. John Pimlott, *The Viking Atlas of World War II* (London: Penguin, 1995), p. 48.
2. Albert Speer, *Inside The Third Reich*, p. 169.
3. Cuenot, *The Herschel Grynszpan Case*, p. 71. The French intelligence files will not be available for public examination until the second decade of the next century.
4. Ibid.

5. Read & Fisher, *Kristallnacht*, p.277.

6. Cuenot, *The Herschel Grynszpan Case*, p. 48.

7. Ibid., p. 49.

8. Read & Fisher, *Kristallnacht*, p.2, have a different theory about the gun, basically calling it a scare gun used by postmen to ward off dogs that chased their bicycles! Needless to say, I disagree with this.

9. Cuenot, *The Herschel Grynszpan Case*, p. 50.

10. Ibid., p. 51.

CHAPTER SIX

1. Fischer, *Nazi Germany: A New History*, pp. 158-9.

2. Schwab, *The Day the Holocaust Began*, p. 20.

3. Translation of document 374-PS, the Wiener Library.

4. Read & Fisher, *Kristallnacht*, p. 84.

5. Schwab, *The Day the Holocaust Began*, p. 27.

6. Arthur Miller, *Broken Glass* (London: Methuen, 1994), p. 17.

7. Read & Fisher, *Kristallnacht*, p. 88. 'In all, about 300 arrests of non-Jews were made, but only about thirty people were detained and sent to the concentration camps.' See also Cuenot, *The Herschel Grynszpan Case*, p. 81.

8. Cuenot, *The Herschel Grynszpan Case*, p. 84.

9. Read & Fisher, *Kristallnacht*, p. 138.

10. Cuenot, *The Herschel Grynszpan Case*, p. 82.

11. Read & Fisher, *Kristallnacht*, p. 137.

12. Resistance against Hitler within all the armed forces was muted but stiff. As early as 2 February 1938, Hitler saw fit to replace with more sympathetic figures the Commander in Chief of the Navy, Erich Raeder; von Fritsch of the army was replaced by von Brauchitsch; and overall command of the armed forces Hitler took for himself from von Blomberg. The next day Ribbentrop replaced (the more aristocratic and aloof) von Neurath as Foreign Minister. (Albert Speer, *Inside The Third Reich*, p.164.)

One of the leaders of the military resistance, Ludwick Beck (Chief of the General Staff until this date), wrote as follows after Kristallnacht:

> It is now a question of final decisions affecting the fate of the nation. History will hold these leaders guilty if they do not act in accordance with their professional and political conscience ... If they all act with a united will, then it will be impossible to make war. In this way, they will have saved their Fatherland from the worst, from catastrophe.

Hitler had Beck murdered in 1944. Eberhard Zeller, *The Flame of Freedom: The German Struggle Against Hitler* (Colorado: Westview Press, 1994), p. 3.

13. Cuenot, *The Herschel Grynszpan Case*, p. 84 op cit.

14. Ibid., p. 85.

15. Ibid.

16. Albert Speer, *Inside The Third Reich*, p.169.

17. Cuenot, *The Herschel Grynszpan Case*, p. 86.

18. Fischer, *Nazi Germany: A New History*, p. 385. Fischer calls 1935 'the seminal year for racial hygiene.'

19. Cuenot, *The Herschel Grynszpan Case*, p. 89.

20. Ibid., p. 77.

21. Schwab, *The Day the Holocaust Began*, p. 25.

22. Cuenot, *The Herschel Grynszpan Case*, p. 78. He is quoting from a story filed by the American journalist, Dorothy Thompson.

23. Schwab, *The Day the Holocaust Began*, p. 116. He thinks that the money did exist, and assumes that a relative must have somehow smuggled it out:

> Herschel and his uncle would deny the existence of any such fund, since they presumably did not want to hand Nazi authorities yet another weapon to use against the family. Furthermore, the persons who assisted in the transfer of the funds were perhaps still under Nazi control.

This belongs in the 'Well they would say that, wouldn't they' category. The fact is, it is difficult to imagine how the money was spirited out of Germany (Schwab does not offer the name of a courier).

24. Read & Fisher, *Kristallnacht*, p. 24.

25. Fischer (*Nazi Germany: A New History*) points out that the vast majority of Nazis were male.

CHAPTER SEVEN

1. Cuenot, *The Herschel Grynszpan Case*, p. 57.

2. Ibid., p. 54. It was the other receptionist, Kreuger, who claimed Herschel said this.

3. Schwab, *The Day the Holocaust Began*, p. 10. Schwab says here that the second bullet lodged in the left shoulder, which is clearly an error (he claims three pages earlier that it was in fact the right).

4. Cuenot, *The Herschel Grynszpan Case*, p. 57, op cit.

5. Ibid., p. 58.

6. Brandt, incidentally, was head of the 'Reich Committee for the Scientific Registration of Serious Hereditary and Congenital Illnesses'. That is a shameless and grand-sounding name for the bunch of butchers who administered Hitler's newly introduced euthanasia programme, which eventually murdered over 100,000 people. Fischer describes the work of this body as follows (Fischer, *Nazi Germany: A New History*, p. 389):

> This committee served as a clearinghouse for reports sent in by physicians and midwives asking what to do about cases involving serious deformities. The reports were then scored by three doctors with a red plus sign (= death), a blue minus sign (= survival), or a question mark in doubtful cases requiring further assessment. Children who had been marked with a red plus sign were then killed by lethal injection.

7. Cuenot, *The Herschel Grynszpan Case*, p. 54.

8. Ibid., p. 56. As far as I can determine, it would have been

nigh on impossible for the Germans to demand Herschel's extradition. Cuenot thinks, though, that 'it was not excluded that the German government could demand the extradition of the slayer.' But the fact that they never did surely underlines my arguument.

9. Cuenot, *The Herschel Grynszpan Case*, p. 54.

10. Ibid., p. 52.

11. Ibid., p. 54 op cit. In keeping with his low opinion of Herschel's personality, Cuenot takes this opportunity to call the boy a fabulist, stating that the 3000 francs existed only in his imagination. The idea that Herschel was a Nazi stooge sprang from the rumour of this money, since the Germans alone could authorise such exports of funds. An anonymous note found by the Nazis in de Moro Giafferi's office after the invasion of France sums up the atmosphere of slander and rumour around the time of the shooting. It is most interesting for what it claims about vom Rath (ibid., p 77):

> Grynszpan was a tool of the Nazis. Van der Lubbe [supposed Reichstag arsonist] also had a Polish Nazi informer at his side ... Grynszpan was also encouraged by agents of Goebbels to assassinate vom Rath. Vom Rath was anti-Nazi, a friend of the Jews, and the Nazis detested him. He knew too much and had to be done away with, one way or another. The object of the Nazis was to kill two birds with one stone, to get rid of vom Rath and the Jews with their money ... Hitler's doctors arranged matters so that vom Rath would not recover. In accord with their program, they did away with this troublesome witness and at the same time had a pretext for their pogroms.

This is a remarkable letter. The reason I have not included it in the body of the text is that, being anonymous, it is not much use as evidence.

12. Ibid., p. 52 op cit.

13. Ibid., p. 53.

14. Ibid., p. 53 op cit.

15. Ibid.

16. Ibid., p. 59.

17. Ibid. I cannot understand why, when all the evidence is pointing towards it, Cuenot will not for a moment countenance any skullduggery by the Nazis.

18. Ruth Andreas-Friedrichs, a member of the anti–Nazi underground, drew some interesting parallels in her diary (published as *Der Schattenman* and in English as *Berlin Underground* [London: Latimer House, 1946]) between vom Rath and an earlier Nazi martyr, Horst Wessel:

> Berlin, Tuesday 8 November 1938
> The evening papers report that some Jewish emigrant has shot a member of the German embassy in Paris. Some claim the matter has political ramifications, that it is an act of revenge of victimised Jewry against the Nazi regime.
> Others suggest a homosexual affair, blackmail, jealousy. Of a second Horst Wessel case. They covered him with laurels, killed thousands of communists in his name, burnt the Reichstag, named squares, streets and regiments after him (Horst Wessel), even celestial hosts ... The day of his death is a national holiday, his battle song the national anthem. Nothing was spared to elevate the erstwhile student to the status of national socialist sainthood. But all this passionate propaganda has failed to cleanse their hero of the suspicion that in his private life he was a rather disreputable character. A lowlifer whose death was not connected with the honour of Germany but with a particular kind of sexual behavior ... Was he a hero or a pimp? Then the communists, not the Jews. Yesterday a pimp – today a homosexual. Perhaps it's just a rumour – but the fact that someone's thought it worthwhile planting it (then as now) shows how it's making the rounds ... that it's in the air.

What is astonishing about this is the fact that the whisper of homo-sexual intrigue is abroad in Germany on 8 November, even before vom Rath was dead.

19. Fischer, *Nazi Germany: A New History*, p. 254: 'Joachim von Ribbentrop, an empty and pretentious social climber who was try-ing to graft himself onto the Nazi bandwagon through his wealthy social connections.'

20. Cuenot, *The Herschel Grynszpan Case*, p. 61.

CHAPTER EIGHT

1. Cuenot, *The Herschel Grynszpan Case*, p. 90.
2. Ibid., p. 91.
3. Ibid.
4. Read & Fisher, *Kristallnacht*, p. 166.
5. Ibid., p. 161.
6. Schwab, *The Day the Holocaust Began*, p. 34.
7. Peter Kurth, *American Cassandra: The Life of Dorothy Thompson* (New York: Little, Brown & Co., 1990), p. 156.
8. Ibid., p. 161.
9. Dorothy Thompson, *Let The Record Speak* (London: Hamish Hamilton, 1939), pp. 2-3.
10. Peter Kurth, *American Cassandra: The Life of Dorothy Thompson*, pp. 161-2.
11. Ibid., p. 202.
12. New York Times, 27 August 1934, quoted in Peter Kurth, *American Cassandra: The Life of Dorothy Thompson*, ibid., p. 203.
13. Speech delivered 25 October 1934, ibid., p. 204.
14. From radio broadcast (*On The Record* on *General Electric Hour*, 18 February 1938), ibid., p. 241.
15. Dorothy Thompson, *Let The Record Speak*, pp. 259-60.
16. Schwab, *The Day the Holocaust Began*, p. 35.
17. Ibid., p. 89.
18. Ibid., & p. 138.

19. Cuenot, *The Herschel Grynszpan Case*, p. 97.

20. Schwab, *The Day the Holocaust Began*, p. 90.

CHAPTER NINE

1. Cuenot, *The Herschel Grynszpan Case*, p. 93.

2. Ibid.

3. Ibid., p. 94.

4. Schwab, *The Day the Holocaust Began*, pp. 85-6. Apparently a Grynszpan ancestor had once disgraced the family by getting a parking ticket.

5. Ibid., p. 100.

6. Cuenot, *The Herschel Grynszpan Case*, p. 103.

7. Ibid.

8. Ibid. p. 115. By this point, Cuenot is really gunning for Herschel ('According to the experts, he did not lack for intelligence. But what is intelligence?').

9. Ibid., p. 98.

10. Schwab, *The Day the Holocaust Began*, p. 101.

11. Ibid.

12. Cuenot, *The Herschel Grynszpan Case*, p. 104.

13. Ibid., p. 99. The possible damage inflicted on the perception of the defence by the jury might easily have been outweighed by sensational publicity.

14. Ibid., p.101 op cit.

15. Schwab, *The Day the Holocaust Began*, p. 188.

16. Cuenot, *The Herschel Grynszpan Case*, p. 107.

17. Ibid., p. 108. 'Eichmann, testifying at his trial in Jerusalem about an interview that he had with [Herschel], was struck by his aggressiveness which remained intact in spite of his long incarceration.'

18. Ibid.

CHAPTER TEN

1. Schwab, *The Day the Holocaust Began*, p. 90. The German embassy was supposedly quoting 'unidentified French legal circles'.

2. Ibid., p. 115. My summation.

3. Cuenot, *The Herschel Grynszpan Case*, p. 121.

4. Schwab, *The Day the Holocaust Began*, p 111.

5. Ibid., p. 112.

6. Ibid.

7. Ibid., p. 114. Relations between Germany and Poland by this time were strained anyway, to say the least.

8. Ibid., pp. 120-1.

9. Ibid. p. 116. My interpretaion: Schwab does not say so, but if Carpe loaded the gun, the premeditation becomes a more difficult, though by no means impossible, fact for the prosecution to prove.

10. Ibid., p. 119. The French in fact sought to bring the case before the courts martial, which were held in camera, so that anti-Nazi feeling in France could not jeopardise Herschel's conviction. This idea was abandoned since vom Rath's representative (by this time Guinand) would be barred from attending.

11. Cuenot, *The Herschel Grynszpan Case*, p. 123.

12. Schwab, *The Day the Holocaust Began*, p 119 op cit.

CHAPTER ELEVEN

1. John Pimlott, *The Viking Atlas of World War II*, p. 54.

2. Schwab, *The Day the Holocaust Began*, p 125.

3. Ibid.

4. Cuenot, *The Herschel Grynszpan Case*, p. 123.

5. Ibid., p. 124.

6. Fischer, *Nazi Germany: A New History*, p. 453.

7. Cuenot, *The Herschel Grynszpan Case*, p. 128. This chapter is mostly based on Cuenot's account of events, with the proviso that I disagree at almost every turn with his interpretation of events.

8. Ibid., p. 125.
9. Ibid.
10. Ibid.
11. Ibid p. 130.
12. Ibid.
13. Schwab, *The Day the Holocaust Began*, p. 128.
14. Cuenot, *The Herschel Grynszpan Case*, p. 129.
15. Ibid., p. 126.
16. Ibid.
17. Ibid., p. 129 op cit.

CHAPTER TWELVE

1. Cuenot, *The Herschel Grynszpan Case*, p. 131.
2. Schwab, *The Day the Holocaust Began*, p 131.
3. Cuenot, *The Herschel Grynszpan Case*, p. 133.
4. Ibid., p. 149.
5. See Susan Sontag, 'Notes On Camp', in *The Susan Sontag Reader* (London: Penguin, 1982), pp. 105-120. This essay remains, to my mind, the best take on the subject.
6. Fischer, *Nazi Germany: A New History*, pp. 230-1.
7. Cuenot, *The Herschel Grynszpan Case*, p. 133 op cit.
8. Ibid., p. 132.
9. Fischer, *Nazi Germany: A New History*, p. 483.
10. Ibid., p. 491. Two Czech agents trained in England parachuted into the country and lobbed a grenade into Heydrich's car. The Nazi managed to leap out, seemingly unhurt, and shoot at them with his pistol. Then he dropped dead. The upholstery springs from the car seats blown apart in the explosion had corkscrewed through his body, piercing and strangulating his insides. Not pleasant, but too good a death for him.
11. Cuenot, *The Herschel Grynszpan Case*, p. 143.
12. Schwab, *The Day the Holocaust Began*, p. 132.
13. Cuenot, *The Herschel Grynszpan Case*, p. 139.

14. Ibid.

15. Ibid.

16. Schwab, *The Day the Holocaust Began*, p. 134.

17. Cuenot, *The Herschel Grynszpan Case*, p. 149.

18. Ibid., pp. 147-8.

19. Schwab, *The Day the Holocaust Began*, p. 171.

20. Cuenot, *The Herschel Grynszpan Case*, p. 137.

21. Ibid., p. 136.

22. Ibid.

23. Schwab, *The Day the Holocaust Began*, p. 172.

24. Ibid., p. 171 op cit.

25. Ibid., p. 172.

26. Read & Fisher, *Kristallnacht*, p. 278.

27. Cuenot, *The Herschel Grynszpan Case*, p. 150.

28. Ibid., p. 151.

29. Read & Fisher, *Kristallnacht*, p. 279. Read and Fisher, in contradistinction to Cuenot, assume that it was the homosexual scandal that put paid to the trial.

30. Schwab, *The Day the Holocaust Began*, p. 186.

31. Read & Fisher, *Kristallnacht*, p. 279 op cit.

CHAPTER THIRTEEN

1. Cuenot, *The Herschel Grynszpan Case*, p. 153.

2. Schwab, *The Day the Holocaust Began*, p. 197.

3. Cuenot, *The Herschel Grynszpan Case*, p. 153 op cit.

4. Schwab, *The Day the Holocaust Began*, p. 198.

5. Cuenot, *The Herschel Grynszpan Case*, p. 156.

6. Schwab, *The Day the Holocaust Began*, p. 199.

7. Cuenot, *The Herschel Grynszpan Case*, p. 158.

8. Ibid., appended letter (no page number).

9. Ibid., p. 160.

10. Ibid., p. 161.

11. Ibid., p. 156 op cit.

12. Schwab, *The Day the Holocaust Began*, p 198 op cit.
13. Ibid., p. 193.
14. Cuenot, *The Herschel Grynszpan Case*, p. 133.

BIBLIOGRAPHY

– Andreas-Friedrichs, Ruth, *Der Schattenman* – Berlin
   Underground) (London: Latimer House, 1946)
– Cuenot, Dr Alain, *L'Affaire Grynszpan-Vom Rath*, trans. David
   Rome (1982) as *The Herschel Grynszpan Case* (Unpublished
   manuscript, Wiener Library, London)
– Fischer, Klaus P., *Nazi Germany: A New History*
   (London: Constable, 1995)
– Kurth, Peter, *American Cassandra: The Life of Dorothy Thompson*
   (New York: Little, Brown & Co., 1990)
– Miller, Arthur, *Broken Glass* (London: Methuen, 1994)
– Pimlott, John, *The Viking Atlas of World War II*
   (London: Penguin, 1995)
– Read, Anthony, and Fisher, David, *Kristallnacht*
   (London: Michael Joseph, 1989)
– Schwab, Gerald, *The Day the Holocaust Began*
   (New York: Praeger, 1990)
– Sontag, Susan, 'Notes On Camp', in *The Susan Sontag Reader*
   (London: Penguin, 1982)
– Speer, Albert, *Inside The Third Reich* (London: Orion, 1995)
– Thompson, Dorothy, *Let The Record Speak* (London:
   Hamish Hamilton, 1939)
– Zeller, Eberhard, *The Flame of Freedom: The German Struggle
   Against Hitler* (Colorado: Westview Press, 1994)

List of Works Consulted

– Arendt, Hannah, *The Origins of Totalitarianism* (New York: Meridian, 1958)
– Bullock, Alan, *Hitler: A Study In Tyranny* (London: Odhams, 1954)
– Fry, Varian, *Surrender on Demand* (New York: Random House, 1945)
– Gilbert, Martin, *The Holocaust* (London: Collins, 1986)
– Kochan, Lionel, *Pogrom, November 10, 1938* (London André Deutsch, 1957)
– Lochner, Louis P., *The Goebbels Diaries* (New York: Doubleday & Co, 1948)
– Marrus, Michael, 'The Strange Story of Herschel Grynszpan', in *The American Scholar* (Winter, 1988)
– Shirer, William, L, *The Rise & Fall of the Third Reich* (New York: Simon & Schuster, 1960)
– Von Hassell, Ulrich, *The Von Hassell Diaries: The Story of the Forces Against Hitler Inside Germany, 1938-1944* (Colorado: Westview Press, 1994)

INDEX

ABOUT THE AUTHOR

Andy Marino gained a first class honours degree in Literature and was awarded his Ph.D. at the age of twenty-five. He has lectured in English and Philosophy at American, Swedish and British universities, but left academia three years ago to live and work in London. He has written a book on the novels of Norman Mailer, Saul Bellow and Philip Roth, and is now researching one on Martin Amis. He is currently writing his first screenplay. Andy Marino is thirty years old.